The Myth of Work–Life Balance

The Myth of Work–Life Balance

The Challenge of Our Time for Men, Women and Societies

Richenda Gambles
Department of Social Policy and Social Work
University of Oxford, UK

Suzan Lewis
Department of Psychology
Manchester Metropolitan University, UK

and

Rhona Rapoport
Institute of Family and Environmental Research
London, UK

John Wiley & Sons, Ltd

Copyright © 2006   John Wiley & Sons Ltd, The Atrium, Southern Gate, Chichester,
West Sussex PO19 8SQ, England

Telephone (+44) 1243 779777

Email (for orders and customer service enquiries): cs-books@wiley.co.uk
Visit our Home Page on www.wiley.com

Other Wiley Editorial Offices

John Wiley & Sons Inc., 111 River Street, Hoboken, NJ 07030, USA

Jossey-Bass, 989 Market Street, San Francisco, CA 94103-1741, USA

Wiley-VCH Verlag GmbH, Boschstr. 12, D-69469 Weinheim, Germany

John Wiley & Sons Australia Ltd, 42 McDougall Street, Milton, Queensland 4064, Australia

John Wiley & Sons (Asia) Pte Ltd, 2 Clementi Loop #02-01, Jin Xing Distripark, Singapore 129809

John Wiley & Sons Canada Ltd, 22 Worcester Road, Etobicoke, Ontario, Canada M9W 1L1

Wiley also publishes its books in a variety of electronic formats. Some content that appears in print may not
be available in electronic books.

Library of Congress Cataloging-in-Publication Data

Gambles, Richenda.
    The Myth of Work-Life Balance: The Challenge of Our Time for Men,
Women and Societies / Richenda Gambles, Suzan Lewis, and Rhona Rapoport.
       p.   cm.
    Includes bibliographical references and index.
    ISBN-13: 978-0-470-09460-0 (cloth : alk. paper)
    ISBN-10: 0-470-09460-5 (cloth : alk. paper)
    ISBN-13: 978-0-470-09461-7 (pbk. : alk. paper)
    ISBN-10: 0-470-09461-3 (pbk. : alk. paper)
  1. Work and family.   2. Men–Employment.   3. Women–Employment.   I. Lewis, Suzan.
II. Rapoport, Rhona.   III. Title.
    HD4904.25.G36 2006
    306.3′61–dc22

                                                                    2005025327

British Library Cataloguing in Publication Data

A catalogue record for this book is available from the British Library

ISBN-13 978-0-470-09460-0 (ppc) 978-0-470-09461-7 (pbk)
ISBN-10 0-470-09460-5 (ppc) 0-470-09461-3 (pbk)

Typeset in 10/12 pt Times by SNP Best-set Typesetter Ltd., Hong Kong
Printed and bound in Great Britain by Antony Rowe Ltd, Chippenham, Wiltshire
This book is printed on acid-free paper responsibly manufactured from sustainable forestry in which at least
two trees are planted for each one used for paper production.

To all our families and all our friends

Contents

About the Authors

Richenda Gambles is currently working as a Lecturer in the Department of Social Policy and Social Work at the University of Oxford, UK. As well as being an Associate of the Work–Life Research Centre, she has been involved with the Institute of Family and Environmental Research as a Research Associate and has worked at the Open University as an Associate Lecturer. She has also worked as a journalist. She has a degree in Social Policy and a masters degree in Gender and Social Policy, both from the London School of Economics.

Suzan Lewis is Professor of Organisational and Work–Life Psychology at Manchester Metropolitan University, UK, a director of the multi-site Work–Life Research Centre and was formerly Visiting Professor at the School of Management, UMIST. She has a degree in Psychology and a PhD in Organisational Psychology. Her research focuses on workplace practice, culture and change in different social policy contexts. She has led many national and international research projects on these topics and is currently directing a European Union funded eight-country study on gender, parenthood and well-being in changing European workplaces. She has published extensively including *The Work Family Challenge*, edited with her son, Jeremy Lewis (1996) and *Work–Life Integration: Case Studies of Organisational Change*, with C. Cooper (2005). She is also a founding editor of the international journal *Community, Work and Family*, published by Taylor & Francis. She has advised governments and worked with employers and policy makers in Britain, the USA and Japan, undertaking consultancy and research on work-life issues.

Rhona Rapoport was director of the Institute of Family and Environmental Research from 1977 until its closure at the beginning of 2005. In addition, for over 20 years she has been a consultant to the Ford Foundation working on affirmative action issues and work and family issues in the United States and in 'developing' countries, and in 1994–1995 she was a scholar in residence at the Ford Foundation. During the 1990s, she was also Distinguished Fellow and adviser at the Center for Gender in Organizations at the Simmons Graduate School of Management in Boston. She has a degree in Social Science from the University of Cape Town, South Africa and a PhD in Sociology from the London School of Economics, which was based on work done in Uganda for two years. A major concern in her work is the issue of equity between men and women. She has collaborated with action research projects in the USA and the UK as well as with a training programme on organisational change and work-family issues for advancing diverse groups in South Africa. She has published extensively over the past 50 years, often with her husband Robert. These publications include *Dual Career Families* (1971) and *Leisure and the Family Life Cycle* (1975). In 2004, she was awarded The Work Life Legacy award by the Families and Work Institute in New York. She has also won an award from the European Work–Life and Diversity Council.

Foreword

The challenges of combining paid work with other parts of life are only too familiar to me. Some years back, I was faced with a dilemma. I loved my job – as U.S. Secretary for Labor, under the Clinton Administration – but it was consuming me. I found I had less and less time or energy for my family and friends. I even began to lose touch with myself. But one night something happened: my son made a comment about wanting to know I was there. I was jolted, taken aback: the consequences of ever-demanding work expectations suddenly so aware to me. But things felt hopeless. How could I, even in my position, expect to make changes to workplace cultures when I was in a job that was eating away at my time, energy and sense of self? I took the only path that seemed open to me. I quit my job. I was lucky. I had the financial resources available to do this and the confidence that I would soon find another job which would place fewer time and energy demands on me. But not everyone has this security: in fact, throughout the world, very few people do.

In this book, Richenda Gambles, Suzan Lewis and Rhona Rapoport explore many of the difficulties men and women from a number of very diverse countries have in combining paid work with other important or meaningful parts of their lives. Through personal stories and discussion of research, they offer a rich account of the multiple reasons why people become so hooked into paid work, and how this affects the time and space remaining available for family, friends, communities, time for leisure and care of self. They also highlight how globalisation pressures make these dilemmas more acute. But they go further than simply description, and raise difficult questions that need to be asked if things are to change.

They argue that government and workplace policies, such as paid parental and other forms of care leaves or flexibility in working times, are important, which is something we in America lag well behind on, particularly when considering some of our European neighbours. But more importantly, the authors emphasise the need to go beyond policies that accommodate certain individuals to merely make *adaptations* to their paid work arrangements. These adaptations can be seen as quick fixes as they do not change actual workplace cultures and everyday practices. So men and (mainly) women making use of them are seen as 'different', 'less committed' and often marginalised at work as a result.

The authors argue powerfully that if people feel a life made up of a myriad of life-sustaining and enriching aspects is a goal to work towards, then there is a need to consider effective policies but also to deal with implementation gaps between policy and behaviour. Inherent in this is the biggest challenge: that of changing mindsets and changing values. In particular, the authors argue that there is a need for collective reflection about assumptions that economic growth – regardless of the personal or social costs – is the main consideration for workplace organisations, society, and many individuals. And they raise important questions about how people can participate in changing mindsets at collective levels.

I know from personal experience that this kind of change can often feel impossible. So I very much welcome this book. It urges us to reflect on the actions we take as individuals, but as individuals who are part of workplace organisations and other institutions in society who can only make real changes in collective and collaborative ways.

Robert B. Reich
University Professor of Social and Economic Policy,
Brandeis University and former U.S. Secretary of Labor

Foreword

The title of this book is particularly apt for a country like India, where the concept of balance is literally a thing of the past. Today, in the land of Yoga, Meditation and Spirituality, there seems to be a lack of balance everywhere – between work and leisure, religion and living, rural and urban and between men and women. That's why this book is so important for a country like India. It gives readers an opportunity to look into their own lives and start questioning the impact of 'progress' in the garb of material gains and increased income. As well as inviting people to challenge the very notion of 'work–life balance' – which is a relatively new concept in India – it encourages readers to reflect on 'work–life' challenges in much more fundamental ways.

India is still a relatively traditional society. The caste system still exists and hierarchical systems are all pervasive. In the land which had a woman Prime Minister way back in the early seventies, there is a huge distinction between men and women even though in ancient literature 'the wife and husband, being equal halves of one substance, are equal in every respect, therefore both should join and take equal part in all work, religious and secular'. Today, the demographics of the Indian workforce are changing, albeit very slowly in the rural areas but by leaps and bounds in urban India. Not only have women joined the workforce in large numbers but with rapid globalisation and competition, paid work has become central to their lives. The book brings out various aspects of India which have been relatively obscured: the materialism of the burgeoning middle class which is ready to spend and not save, the decline of the joint family system which was the mainstay of Indian society, and the increased loneliness and alienation that people in the workforce are going through in the name of 'progress'. These issues, highlighted by the authors, bring out the fact that a country like India which has a rich tradition of a huge support system of extended families, friends and paid help (who ended up as loyal family retainers) is fast disintegrating into a confused society. The need to compete in a global economy and the pressures to do so in 'western ways' are actually destroying the social fabric of India. The authors encourage the readers to think of ways to progress within the circumference of one's own traditional institutions of families, communities and societies.

Another fascinating feature of the book is a look into the new sector emerging in India, called the Information Technology Enabled Services (ITES). Since India is coming to be known as a hub for Information Technology, this book becomes even more important. It unfolds the trials and tribulations of the younger workforce as they grapple with working against their biological rhythms to take advantage of the time differential with the west. The authors, with in-depth interviews and observations bring out hitherto hidden issues of alienation and problems in mental and physical health of the young men and women (with an average age of 24) who work during the night and sleep during the day, all in the name of progress and growth. They unveil the havoc that these working patterns are creating and highlight the difficult battle to maintain time and energy for multiple parts of life.

What I find most interesting about 'The Myth of Work–Life Balance' is the multi-country backdrop of the book, against which each country's canvas unfolds – all very different from each other with a common underlying theme of difficulties people face in harmonising paid work with other parts of life, despite the unique and inherent strengths and weaknesses of each country. The authors get the readers to speculate on issues of policy and show very clearly that policies aren't enough. These challenges are intricately fused with attitudes, beliefs and expectations of individuals, families, organisations, communities and societies. The book urges policy makers of each country to start thinking about feelings and the multiple needs and pressures of its own people which must be considered if implementation and use of these policies is to be effective. For India, this book is a well of knowledge where our policy makers can clearly see that importing new policies and legislation from the western world is not in itself a sufficient solution.

I welcome this book because it is about real people from across the globe, where everyone is a stakeholder in the challenges of combining the many parts of life. The authors are highly successful in pushing people to think in holistic and collaborative ways to seek some answers to very difficult and challenging questions.

Dr Tripti P. Desai
Associate Professor and Head of Organisational Behaviour and Human
Resource Management, Institute for Integrated Learning in Management
New Delhi, India

Acknowledgements

The research on which this book is based was called 'Looking Backwards to go Forward' in the field relating paid work to other parts of life. This 'field' has been around for about four decades but people take a long time to hear certain things that go against conventional mindsets. The Ford Foundation had supported earlier research in this area, some of which was reported in the publication *Beyond Work-Family Balance: Enhancing Gender Equity and Work Performance* (Rapoport, Bailyn, Fletcher, & Pruitt, 2002). We wish to give special thanks to those who were in the Foundation and had the foresight to support the work in this 'field', including Susan Berresford, Constance Buchanan and June Zeitlin. The study on which this book is based was made possible by a grant from the Ford Foundation to the Institute of Family and Environmental Research. In addition, the Japan Foundation, the Great Britain Sasakawa Foundation and Manchester Metropolitan University helped to support our scenario meeting that took place at the end of the active research phase.

There are many, many people who have contributed to our thinking and the development of this project. Our interviewees, members of the country meetings, and those who attended the scenario meeting at the end cannot be named for confidentiality reasons but we wish to thank them for their invaluable help. We also wish to thank those who helped us in other capacities: in particular we would like to acknowledge Tripti Desai (India), Laura Den Dulk (The Netherlands), Ellen Galinsky (USA), Lisa Harker (UK), Bram Peper (The Netherlands), Betty Pruitt (USA), Hiroki Sati (Japan), Ragnhild Sohlberg (Norway), Ria Smidt (South Africa), Anneka Van Den Huiskes (The Netherlands) and Caroline White (UK) who organised country meetings and/or helped us with country timelines and locating people for our interviews. We are grateful to Barbara Heinzen and Hardin Tibbs, who facilitated the international scenario meeting. Finally, we appreciate the opportunity to go on a retreat to write parts of this book at the C'an Pujola Foundation in Majorca. Many people have also read parts or the whole of the manuscript and offered challenging but always encouraging feedback. Thanks to Lotte Bailyn, David Bonbright, Marcie Pitt-Catsouphes, Ellen Galinsky, Judy Fraser, Lorna Rapoport, Herta von Stiegel and two anonymous reviewers.

The work done by the three of us on this book reflects the fact that we cover almost three generations – both in the life course and in the history and approach to the topics with which we are concerned. This has meant that we have had a diverse perspective all the way through. This diversity has great strengths but also involves working through different ways of looking at the same things, reflecting, in part, some of the challenges – and opportunities – we discuss throughout this book. This book reflects a collaborative piece in thought, word and deed. At times it has been difficult, but always rewarding. So thanks from each of us to each other without whom none of this work could or would have been possible.

'There is no wealth but life'

John Ruskin, 1860, *Unto This Last*

Global Stories from the Front Line

Harmonising paid work with other parts of life is difficult for Zhilah in **South Africa**. Her daughter is dying of AIDS; as well as dealing with her own grief, she is dealing with the consequences of being a carer to her young grandchildren. She has been taking so much leave from work recently that her employers are getting impatient and she fears she will lose her job. She loves her grandchildren and wants to be there for them. But she also loves her job. During the apartheid era there were few opportunities for someone like her. But post-apartheid, affirmative action programmes have given her a chance and she has been doing really well.

Many people are unemployed and looking for work. If she loses her job, will she be able to get another? Will she find a new job that enables her to combine it with looking after young children? She is anxious that if she does not find work, she may have to return to her husband and be financially dependent on him again. Although they have somewhat made their peace and see each other more regularly, she fears that if she returns to live with him the violence may begin again. Sometimes she allows herself to fantasise that they will be reunited. Perhaps, she muses, he will cut down on his paid work and share some of the care of their grandchildren, enabling her to have a job too and the power that an income in her own right would bring. But she knows this will not happen. Her husband sees childcare as woman's work and moreover, given his past history of violence, she does not trust him with the grandchildren. Aside from these fears and anxieties, she knows there has been a spate of changes from permanent to temporary work at the goldmine where he works and there are few concessions for leaves or shorter hours. Conditions are bad and he will say he cannot afford to jeopardise his already precarious job.

Johan in **The Netherlands** has many workplace pressures and demands; but he is trying to take on more responsibility for the children to enable his wife to work part-time. He has negotiated flexibility to leave work early on Mondays and Tuesdays so that he can pick up his eldest son from school and to make his hours up later in the week. His wife, Anna, however, has been experiencing a lot of pressure at work herself recently and frequently asks if he can help her out more with various tasks as and when they arise. She wants him to reduce his hours and also work part-time. Their friends Tanja and Hans have this kind of arrangement, but Hans works in the public sector, where there seems to be more accommodation for couples who both want to work part-time and share child-care. Johan knows there is less accommodation for such arrangements in his own workplace.

He is also concerned about the amount Anna is working at the moment. She is busy on a project with US clients and, although she is contracted to work three days a week, she works much more. She often stays up late replying to emails and dealing with the extra work this inevitably entails. On her 'days off' she tends to continue her work from home. She has been saying how stressed and exhausted she feels. She needs to be careful – Johan is well aware of the potential consequences of overworking as his sister is currently on stress-related sickness leave. He knows he should do more to help, but what can he do?

Elizabeth, in the **United States of America**, has problems too. She is waiting for replies to a number of urgent emails that she has fired off to Anna, her Dutch colleague, mentioned above. Elizabeth does not have time for this today. Her mother is leaving hospital and moving into a nursing home and Elizabeth has arranged to leave work early that day to go with her mother and help her get settled in. Family matters are normally left to Enrika, her wonderful nanny, who has somewhat saved Elizabeth's career not to mention the generous health care benefits and security her job gives her. Unlike her last nanny, who had to juggle childcare alongside working for Elizabeth, Enrika has no immediate family responsibilities in the USA. Elizabeth no longer has to rush off in crisis moments to attend to the needs of her children and mother, which always provokes disapproving comments from senior colleagues. Apart from the twice yearly visits back home to see her own children, Enrika is always around and so much more reliable. Although Elizabeth recognises that Enrika's problems of combining paid work with family life are so much greater than her own, and occasionally hears her crying in her bedroom, she finds this difficult to dwell on. It is not that she does not care. Rather she cannot cope with the implications.

Today she has a different problem. The clock is ticking. Her mother is waiting. She cannot ask her husband, Tom, to help her out. He is away on business, again, overseeing some of the arrangements for a call centre relocation to India. She allows herself a brief moment to think about him. It feels so long since they have actually spent some quality time together. She picks up the phone to try his mobile, but it goes straight onto voice mail. She leaves a message, and checks her emails again to see if Anna had responded, but still, nothing.

Ravi in **India**, driving home through the relentless Delhi traffic after another long night at the call centre, is – like Elizabeth – thinking about his mother. His wife, Naila called earlier, just before she left for the school where she works as a teacher, to say a letter has arrived saying his mother is sick. Ravi needs to see his mother, but she lives miles away in the village where he grew up. He will have to wait until his scheduled time off: four more days – or nights – to go. Making his way through the crowded lanes, past rickshaws, cows and beggars, he curses his mother for brushing aside his repeated requests for her to come and live with him. He has told her over and again that she should be with him: that his father would have wanted her to be with him. It is his duty to look after her. But his mother always says the city has nothing for her. Despite her son and grandchildren being there, she says it is not what she knows: she does not want to adjust.

Ravi thinks about driving out there, today, to go and pick her up. He could forgo sleep, just this once, but he knows she will not come back with him and instead she will plead with him to stay with her. But he cannot take time off work. There are queues of people waiting to fill his position if he gives any sign of non-commitment. Besides, there is a promotion coming up and he stands a good chance of getting it if he plays his cards right. The promotion would help him and Naila buy the new apartment they have seen. They need the extra money, for their future and their children. It is not so easy swapping shifts either. People have things planned for their days off, they have their own families to see.

Claire, in the **United Kingdom**, also has problems harmonising paid work with other parts of her life. She is working late and has not yet finished her report and is missing out on another evening with her children. She has been distracted by an earlier conversation with David, one of her young trainees recently shifted over to the call centre section. He has heard rumours of outsourcing plans to India and is concerned for his job. He called her earlier to see if she knows anything. Of course she does: the transfer will be finalised in the next day or so. She is just waiting to hear from their US partners, who are currently in India. As a multinational company, they know they have to keep up to be globally competitive. She has seen the figures outlining the long-term savings of the relocation. It makes sense, on paper, yet David's call has shaken her. David and his partner Sally need his income. Sally has a job in a supermarket, but it does not pay well. David has told Claire that childcare demands mean Sally cannot even hope to advance and take on a managerial role because of the unpredictable and longer hours this will entail. What will they do if he loses his job? Claire knows there are no vacancies for David back in her section.

She sympathises with them, but at the same time she also feels strangely envious of Sally, who spends more time at home, while she, the 'successful' one is missing out on time with her own family. Everyone is talking about 'work–life balance'; it is everywhere, in the newspapers, on the TV, in HR documents that circulate the desks. Yet the pressures at work have been so intense lately and despite all the talk of being a 'family-friendly' company, she is seeing none of the benefits.

Yasuo, in **Japan**, sits on a crowded train to Tokyo, heading for another long day at the office. He is mulling over recent problems with his grown-up children. He is concerned about the future of his youngest son who has recently left his job in the city, saying there is more to life than money. Yasuo feels his son is throwing his life and all the money he has spent on education away.

This is the last thing he needs right now. His elder son, Junichi, with a demanding job that takes him all over the world, has been going through marital difficulties and now his wife, Machiko, has left him. Machiko has long been frustrated because Junichi is away so much, but when she discovered he had been having an affair, that had been the final straw. She has taken their young son and gone to live with a friend. Junichi has confided in Yasuo that Machiko is demanding he spend more time with her and their young child, and less time away, if she is to come back and make another go of things. However, Japan is not like other countries, such as Norway for instance, where Junichi often visits on business. There it seems acceptable for fathers to leave early and take time off when family commitments demand. But not in Japan, where long hours and 100 per cent 'commitment' are expected, especially in a senior position. Yasuo is angry with Machiko for making these demands on his son. Yasuo's own wife is upset by the situation too. When she had married Yasuo all those years ago, they had made a promise to each other that they would be together for life. She cannot understand why Machiko is being like this, and is upset that she now rarely sees her only grandson.

Harmonising paid work with other parts of life is also proving elusive for Per in **Norway**. Per knows of some of the struggles people have in other countries, yet he and his wife Siri are also experiencing difficulties. In Norway things are supposed to be easy. They have publicly funded childcare provision, supportive parental leave policies and, moreover, men like him willing to take a lot of responsibility for the care of children. Over the past few years, however, things have become more difficult. He is in an international section of an oil company, which is going through a period of restructuring and job losses.

He is finding it harder and harder to leave work on time and always takes work home with him.

Per fully shares the responsibility of their children with Siri: always insisting on being just as involved, as well as doing his fair share of household tasks. He knows that Siri, too, is trying to get ahead in her job. The pressures from all sides seem to be taking their toll on both of them, they see less of their friends and wider family, and they are fighting with each other more than before. Norway is supposed to be so progressive, compared with other countries, but they both feel harried and torn in all directions.

   Different contexts, different problems, yet the difficulties facing this small international cast acting out their everyday lives have many similarities and the challenges they confront are more connected than perhaps they realise.

Setting the Scene

CHAPTER 1

A Pivotal Challenge in the Global Context

The opening Prologue stories are based on the lives of real people whom we met in the course of researching this book and reflect some of the challenges people face in combining multiple parts of life. When we consider the complex ways in which they, and others like them, combine and value the different parts of their lives, we argue that contemporary debates or policy initiatives promoting 'work–life balance' or 'work–family reconciliation' seem to only skim the surface of much deeper and more fundamental sets of challenges and constraints. This book explores some of the complex ways in which people are able to prioritise or value various aspects of life in a context in which the demands of paid work and emphasis on its virtues seem to be increasing. We look at the impact of current patterns of paid work on individual well-being and on family, friendship and community experiences. We also explore the connections between contemporary 'work–life' pressures and men and women's identities and male–female relationships. The book focuses on experiences of people in formal paid work, mostly working in the post-industrial knowledge economy.[1] However, these workers do not exist in a vacuum and we also explore some of the ways in which paid work and personal life pressures are experienced by other sectors of society and how this can perpetuate various social inequities. For example, as we saw in the Prologue, the domestic worker employed by Elizabeth's family in the USA also struggles to manage her own complex life while supporting her employers in managing their lives (dilemmas we will return to particularly in the final chapter). Another example in our opening stories is Sally in the UK, who works in a low paid job at a supermarket. She finds she is unable to seek promotion because this may entail extra and unpredictable hours that are incompatible with her care responsibilities.[2]

Below we emphasise and reflect on three critical and related tensions that are connected with challenges people face in combining paid work with other parts of their lives, before discussing the limitations of responses to these challenges that rely on policy alone. We then provide some background to the study on which this book is based and go on to argue that there is a need to move beyond current initiatives and debates about balancing paid

---

[1] We recognise that challenges of harmonising paid work with other parts of life are not limited to these sectors of society. Indeed the challenges are much greater amongst the least privileged and most vulnerable members of society. Our participants are all relatively privileged and although some speak for the less privileged there are many other perspectives and many voices unheard.

[2] See, for example, Crompton and Brockman (2003); see also Toynbee (2003), who discusses some of the difficulties low paid workers have in juggling paid work with care responsibilities and how these struggles can prevent them from seeking work that is better paid and has better conditions.

work with other parts of life, to ask and reflect on bigger questions. Finally we provide a brief overview of the remainder of the book.

CRITICAL TENSIONS

There are three critical and interrelated factors that we believe are central to discussions about 'work–family conflict', 'work–life balance', and what we refer to as harmonising paid work with other parts of life (see Chapter 3).

Firstly, paid work has become increasingly demanding and invasive in people's lives. This may be due, for example, to poverty level pay and the need for multiple jobs; new forms of work and working patterns that put increased pressure on people; the intrinsic satisfaction of some forms of work; or the lure of consumerism and accumulation. Whatever the reasons, the invasiveness of paid work can divert time and energy from other equally important parts of life.

Secondly, time and energy to connect with others and give and receive care – as parents, children, lovers or friends, or even time to care for ourselves – are crucial for individual and societal well-being. Yet these aspects of life can be increasingly squeezed out by current patterns of paid work, or can exclude people with demanding non-paid care responsibilities from much paid work. In the recent past it has tended to be women have who struggled to fit in caring responsibilities and expectations with other activities. Now, as our opening stories illustrate, many men are also struggling to find space in their lives to connect with and care for others across a variety of life situations.

Thirdly, in this context, the ways in which men and women experience and negotiate their roles, identities and relationships with each other are crucial to ways in which paid work and other parts of life are harmonised. But 'choices' about how men and women do this are often constrained by assumptions about what men and women 'should' do and how they 'should' interact with each other. Despite the growth in women's participation in paid work since the 1960s, there remains less reciprocal change among men, particularly in terms of their participation in care and unpaid domestic activities. This impacts on both men and women's experiences and family life.

Many people regard the ways in which work can be harmonised with other parts of life as individual concerns and as a small, rather self-indulgent problem in today's world. In India, for example, we hear that while people are aware that emerging patterns of paid work are damaging some relationships in families and communities, 'bigger' issues of competing globally overshadow these concerns. Some feel that worrying about family relationships and well-being is a luxury they as a society cannot afford to address. In the business world in 'developed' countries, and among many governments, the importance of paid work and the primacy of economic competitiveness, whatever the personal costs, are almost accepted wisdom. Profits and short-term efficiency gains are often placed before social issues of care and human dignity. Yet the three interacting tensions outlined above are exacerbated by increasing economic competition within and between countries. The ways in which people are able to harmonise work with other parts of life are inherently bound up with debates about the current global economy, associated demands in paid work, and equity and well-being dynamics. Difficulties men and women experience in combining paid work with other parts of life can no longer be considered as purely personal, family, employer or even national concerns. They are global challenges.

POLICIES ARE NECESSARY BUT NOT SUFFICIENT

Some governments and some employing organisations have developed policies, varying in type and generosity across different countries and workplaces that aim to make it easier for people – particularly women – to combine paid work with the rest of life. Policies are necessary. Government policy packages, which take different forms at different times and in different contexts, include various combinations of time, service and cash provisions that are essential for supporting all employees, including those who do not work in supportive organisations and the lowest paid and most vulnerable workers. Time provisions, which are also made available through some employer policies, include maternity, parental and family leaves, part-time or flexi-time possibilities. Service provisions include child, elder or other types of care support. In addition, cash provisions include benefits that compensate stay-at-home carers or offer cash resources to buy in a range of supports.

Yet while these policies are crucial, and various types and extents of provisions can have differing consequences on equity between men and women as well as different impacts on adult and child well-being,[3] their overall impact has been limited (see Brandth & Kvande (2001); Lewis (1997); Lewis, S. (2001); Rapoport, Bailyn, Fletcher & Pruitt (2002)). Government policies have to be implemented at the workplace level where they are often undermined by working practices, structures and cultures as well as wider societal norms. Employer policies on flexible working arrangements, for example, are also undermined by these factors.

Policies, while offering varying levels of entitlement and support, tend not to tackle or address cultural and organisational values or deep identity tensions that are so important in implementation. For example, both statutory parental leave entitlements and employer policies on part-time work are more often taken up by women than men, even in countries where father involvement is positively encouraged in policy making. This is due, for example, to assumptions that 'ideal' workers do not modify work for family reasons, alongside notions about what is appropriate behaviour for men and women.[4] The result is that people – usually women – who take up 'work–family' or 'work–life' entitlements tend to be undervalued in workplaces and are often penalised in terms of pay and workplace advancement. What does this say about how various activities are valued? And how might assumptions about 'ideal' workers, or about men and women's appropriate roles, relate to social concerns such as falling birth rates or to an emerging deficit of time available for care? These are the questions we explore in this book.

THE STORY BEHIND THIS BOOK

We, the authors, represent three generations of women who have been experiencing these challenges within our personal and professional lives at different life course phases over a period that, for one of us, spans more than 50 years. During this time, we have witnessed

---

[3] See Gornick and Meyers (2003), in which the authors give a detailed and comparative summary of the impacts of particular policies. For example, they discuss the extent to which longer maternity or parental leaves can impact on women's labour market opportunities as long spells of exclusion can limit human capital; the extent to which shorter leaves may impact on child well-being; and the ways in which different countries offer support for childcare or flexible working. Their study explores different policy provisions and overall country outcomes such as gender equity, child well-being and poverty risks, and they take a critical view of the current US approach.

[4] See footnote 2.

the ways in which families and the nature of work have been changing, and have noted the developments in government and workplace responses together with their impacts and limitations. Our aim here is to reflect on 'work–life' challenges and stimulate further thinking about potential collaborative changes amongst men and women in families, communities, workplace organisations and wider societal contexts that might support the harmonisation of paid work with other parts of life in ways that are potentially more equitable, satisfying and sustainable.

With a grant from the Ford Foundation, for a project we called *Looking Backwards to Go Forwards: Work-personal life integrations in seven countries*, we explored 'work–life' challenges in India, Japan, The Netherlands, Norway, South Africa, the United Kingdom and the United States of America. In this book we draw from these explorations to discuss how situations and ways of thinking about combining paid work with other parts of life have evolved in various countries since the 1950s. We also explore persisting and emerging barriers that appear to hold back more progressive change with a view to thinking about strategies and processes for moving forward in more optimal ways.

We explore the trends and challenges experienced in seven countries with different levels of government or workplace support for harmonising paid work with other parts of life and at varying stages of economic development. We include Norway because of government commitment to equality between men and women backed up by well-established social policies to support the reconciliation of employment and family life. The Netherlands is included as a country that has come more recently to these issues, but is now developing more public policy and public–private initiatives and supports to enable women to be more involved in paid work. The UK is discussed because there is currently a great deal of hype about 'work–life balance' among government, employers and others. Living in the UK, it is also the context we know best. The USA is included as a contrast in that there is minimal social policy support but much attention has been paid to work–life issues at the workplace level. Japan also offers an interesting case. There are long working hours and a culture that tends to espouse particularly 'traditional' notions of what it means to be a man or a woman. Yet there have been recent government policies and drives to change workplaces to make them more 'women' or 'family' friendly, motivated in large part by a dramatic decline in the birth rate. As we are also interested in how these challenges are affecting a 'developing' country connected with the global economy, we include India.[5] The technological revolution taking place in India and the high level of outsourcing of workplaces from 'developed' countries enables us to observe the impact of global mobility from a 'recipient's' perspective. However, India is a very diverse country. It is important to note that we focus mainly on the capital city, New Delhi, and on experiences of people who are more directly connected with new economy developments.[6] Finally, South Africa is also included as a country with mixed levels of economic development, which is being transformed, post-apartheid, and where attention to diversity issues is central to this transformation. Again, our particular focus means that our participants, though diverse, cannot reflect the whole social spectrum.

The Ford Foundation grant was given to stimulate a 'think' piece (rather than an exhaustive piece of empirical work) about the ways in which people are able to harmonise paid

---

[5] We recognise that using the terminology of 'developing' and 'developed' countries is problematic as it implies that developing countries should be working towards and incorporating approaches and strategies adopted in developed contexts. For the sake of clarity, we use the terms 'developing' and 'developed' but place these in inverted commas to remind of the difficulty of these labels and problems that may emanate from using these terms.

[6] This book does not deal with some of the greatest hardships in the poorest countries, such as malnutrition or absolute poverty.

work in the global knowledge economy with other parts of life: to explore what has happened in a range of countries and current situations, and to generate ideas for moving forward. In order to do this we explored the experiences, perspectives and reflections of a range of 'experts' connected in some way or another with contemporary 'work–life' challenges. These experts – whom we refer to as our participants and co-researchers – are connected with issues about harmonising paid work with other parts of life as: academics and researchers; politicians or policy makers; people working at various levels in formal workplace organisations, including public, private and Non-Governmental Organisations (NGOs); external consultants; trade union officials; and journalists. Our participants offered their own grounded insights from experience, research and individual understandings of their own countries, workplaces, families and personal circumstances and collaborated with us in the process of mutual enquiry.

Our research approach is qualitative and our methods were chosen to encourage our co-researchers to engage with us in reflection and collaborative thinking. Norman Denzin and Yvonne Lincoln (1998, p. 3) argue that 'qualitative research involves the studied use and collection of a variety of empirical materials – case study, personal experience, introspective, life story, interview, observational, historical, international and visual texts that describe routine and problematic moments in and meaning in people's lives . . . qualitative researchers deploy a wide range of interconnected methods, hoping always to get a better fix on the subject matter to hand'. We have used a variety of methods for precisely these reasons: to explore past, present and future tensions with our participants in different contexts.

In the course of our research, where possible, we compiled *country timelines* with the help of some of our participants from the different countries, to capture something of the history, and shifting evolutions of harmonising paid work with other parts of life. The compilation of these timelines involved looking at developments since the 1950s, which included relevant legislation, workplace policies and potential and emerging levers for change. The timelines, albeit limited by our perspectives and the perspectives of those who helped construct them, enable us to view the historical process over time.

We also held *country meetings* in some of these countries that were organised and convened by local colleagues who brought together diverse participants whom they knew to be working or engaging with 'work–life' challenges. The aim of these country meetings was to unearth perspectives from a range of people grappling with these challenges to explore what is currently being said and felt in various contexts. In these meetings we encouraged diverse groups of people to reflect on what was going on in their own lives and also more broadly on the country situations and to identify and discuss current debates. As the meetings were convened by local colleagues, the format differed slightly in each country. For example, some lasted for one day, others for two days enabling informal discussion and reflection to take place overnight. We felt that the latter structure was optimal but it was not always feasible.

In addition we held *in-depth interviews* with some of the participants from the country meetings – as well as with some others who did not attend the meetings who were also closely connected with 'work–life' issues in varying ways – so as to generate personal stories and engage in deeper level discussions and thinking.

During this research we were very struck by people's eagerness in all seven countries to talk about experiences and discontents in relation to combining paid work with other parts of life. Yet it was difficult for them – and also for us – to think about how things might change. Assumptions about the primacy of paid work as well as assumptions about particular identities of men and women, and what they 'should' be attached to, are particularly endemic and inherent within conventional 'wisdoms'. This can block creative and unrestrained thinking. Perhaps this is reflective of observations made by Frederic Jameson: that conceptualising beyond capitalism in its current forms has become harder than contemplating life beyond death.[7] It was this seemingly impenetrable impasse that prompted us to embark on a fourth aspect of our study: *an international meeting using scenario techniques*. The aim was to continue our discussions with some of our international participants in collaboration with professional scenario planners. Scenario planning draws lessons about possible futures. This meeting aimed to envision future harmonisations of paid work with other parts of life and to think about creative strategies for more optimal changes at multiple levels – including individual mindsets, families, communities, workplaces and wider society and international levels – that could be disseminated in some way within and across the different countries in our study.

Researchers always have a particular stance towards the questions being asked. As David Silverman (2002, p. 2) puts it, 'whatever we observe is impregnated by our assumptions'. In interpreting our data, we are aware that our own positions – as white, middle-class women, albeit at different stages in our life courses – have influenced what we have probed and focused on, as well as what we document in this book. We come from different academic disciplines in the social sciences but share similar standpoints, including looking at these issues through gender, social justice and sustainability lenses and a focus on processes of change. We set this out in more detail in Chapter 3.

Our topic is huge. Conventional approaches to qualitative research warn against taking on topics that are too big and risk saying a little about a big social issue (see Silverman, 2001). We agree that in-depth analyses of specific issues or problems can help elucidate situations and reveal useful new perspectives and understandings. However, at the same time we argue this can be part of the problem if pursued in isolation. It is the very failure to look at the bigger picture of the ways in which people are able to harmonise paid work with other parts of life that has stopped people from asking taboo questions about, for example, the impact of dominant forms of market practices on people's lives. So, perhaps the first conventional wisdom that we challenge is that research questions need always be small and manageable (though our methods are manageable, including the number of participants that we have been able to engage in the process).

ASKING THE BIG QUESTIONS

As we reflect on the total process of this project we identify 'big' questions connected with the underlying tensions and undercurrents we feel continue to hold back change.

Firstly, there is limited thinking about alternative forms of capitalism that value social needs as much as profit. This is despite what dominant forms of neo-liberal capitalism appear to be doing to the well-being and quality of life of people in many societies. How do we make systems more responsive to human needs? How might it be possible to really move beyond the conventional wisdom that profits and efficiency are more important than people?

---

[7] Cited in Moss (2003), in which he explores barriers and obstacles for widespread use and implementation of parental leaves and reflects on tensions between ethics of care and ethics of paid work.

Secondly, there is limited thinking about how people who want a 'life' outside the workplace or those who have other needs and responsibilities can be valued in workplaces. How is it possible to overcome the reluctance or even apparent lack of awareness of the need to address workplace structures, cultures and practices that persist in penalising people who make changes in their individual working practices? Is it possible to value diversity of background, skills and ways of working, or to recognise that experiences from all parts of life may enhance relationships in the workplace and overall workplace effectiveness?

Thirdly, despite all that has been written about men, women, femininity and masculinity, there is a lack of widespread thinking about changing identities, changing roles and changing relationships between men and women in the context of harmonising the many parts of life. How is it possible to overcome resistance to thinking about deep identity issues that arise from changing relationships between men and women in different societies? Is it possible to develop widespread awareness of how structures, cultures and practices that shape all levels of society affect and prevent men and women from developing new identities, roles and relationships with each other in ways that enhance experiences of well-being or equity between them?

Fourthly, there is limited thinking about the connections between problems of combining paid work with other parts of life and many other social concerns. How is it possible to overcome the marginalisation of challenges in harmonising paid work with family or personal life and approach these dilemmas in wider and more radical ways?

Finally, there is limited thinking about the actual processes of change. How is it possible to overcome a focus on quick fixes and appreciate and address the complexity of change processes necessary for wider and deeper change?

We appreciate these are normative questions. Yet these are important and big questions that need to be asked at all levels of society; by *individuals* in the everyday organisation of their lives; by *families*, households and people in intimate relationships who value equity, companionship or connectedness with others; by *workplaces* seeking to recruit, retain, motivate and utilise diverse workers; in *communities* hoping to sustain or revive local participation and civic spirit; and *societies as a whole* that need to consider how to respond to changes in families, work, workplaces and communities in an increasingly globally connected world. Such questions and potential solutions require collective – and ongoing – thinking and discussion. Yet in a world characterised by perceived growing individualism and busyness, this seems increasingly difficult.

An important barrier is that many people have difficulty *hearing* the argument that harmonising paid work with other parts of life is connected to many other significant issues facing people and societies today. Approaching the ways people harmonise paid work with other parts of life in wider and more radical ways may be too challenging. It can feel too big, too complex and too difficult to talk about. Talking and thinking about paid work and other parts of life in deeper and more fundamental ways requires people to operate across all levels of society and confront some very basic assumptions and identities. This can feel risky, and so questioning many of the deeper assumptions connected with the harmonisation of paid work with other parts of life – such as assumptions that profits and shareholder value are more important than individual, family or community well-being, or assumptions about men and women's 'proper' roles – are often considered taboo. Nevertheless, in the words of Zygmunt Bauman (1998, p. 5) in his discussion of the human consequences of globalisation: 'questioning the ostensibly unquestionable premises of our way of life is arguably the most urgent service we owe to our fellow humans and our selves'.

OVERVIEW OF THE BOOK

In the next chapter we begin the process of 'looking backwards to go forwards' by exploring potential levers for change since the 1950s, government and workplace responses, and current concerns and emerging potential levers for change in relation to harmonising paid work with other parts of life in the seven countries. We explore some of the changes and developments that have occurred over the last 50 or so years, pulling together what we have heard from our participants alongside insights from relevant research. In Chapter 3 we discuss the need for thinking about change at multiple levels and set out our criteria for optimal change: equity, well-being and sustainability.

In the second part of the book we explore the connections between paid work and other parts of life in more detail in terms of three interrelated themes, mirroring the critical undercurrents identified at the beginning of this chapter. In Chapter 4 we explore experiences of paid work in the current global context. In Chapter 5 we look at experiences of families, communities, friendships and leisure in the context of current experiences of paid work. We then go on, in Chapter 6, to explore some of the connections with these experiences and relationships between men and women, which we feel are critical to this whole set of challenges.

In the final part of the book we begin to think about ways of moving forwards. We discuss possible future scenarios and think about possible strategies for change across multiple levels, that may move us beyond the current 'myth of work–life balance', urging wider collaboration amongst people within and across different societies.

CHAPTER 2

Evolutions and Developments in Seven Countries

This chapter begins the process of 'looking backwards to go forwards' by charting some past and current developments in the seven countries that relate to emerging potential levers for change and government and workplace responses for combining paid work with other parts of life.

People have always combined the different parts of their lives – including paid and unpaid work, family joys and obligations and other caring responsibilities, friendships, leisure and community activities – in some way or another. Looking back, in pre-industrial societies, men tended to be the hunters, explorers or warriors, with the child-bearing role keeping women close to the home. These differences translated into an inferior status for women so that most pre-industrial families and societies were patriarchal and women were largely excluded from the public realm.[1] Yet divisions of labour between men and women were not always rigid. In many pre-industrial societies, women could own property or claim economic return for their labour. They often worked alongside husbands or other male family members and handled business affairs when necessary. Child rearing and other forms of caring or domestic work were integrated into many men and women's daily lives.[2] These patterns continue to be seen in some agrarian sections of contemporary societies.

With the gradual emergence of the Industrial Revolution, separations between paid work and family life became more clearly defined. Paid work became more closely associated with men and family care with women, which interacted with assumptions that stereotypical conventional male behaviour and attributes were more suited to requirements of much paid work and stereotypical behaviour and attributes of women were more suited to domestic and care activities.[3] The separation of paid work and family care, with particular role expectations for men and women, resulted in particular assumptions about harmonising different parts of life. Assumptions about men and women's different roles and

---

[1] See Connell (2001, p. 31) who argues that in the context of Europe, 'historical research suggests that . . . before the 18th century . . . women were certainly regarded as different from men, but different in the sense of being incomplete or inferior examples of the same character (for instance, having less of the faculty of reason). Women and men were not seen as bearers of qualitatively different characters; this conception accompanied the bourgeois ideology of "separate spheres" in the nineteenth century'.

[2] See Rapoport et al. (2002, pp. 25–28) for a lucid summary; see also Hartmann (1979) for a detailed account of the ways in which women were traditionally kept out of much productive work that was away from the domestic setting and the ways in which this developed over time. In particular, she discusses domestic demands on women as well as limited access to apprenticeships reflecting interactions between forces of patriarchy and emerging capitalist exchanges. She also goes on to discuss the ways in which male dominated trade unions also served to keep women in marginal or excluded positions in terms of paid labour so as to protect the levels of wages men were able to command. Other useful discussions include Nancy Cott (1977) and John Demos (1986, pp. 43–45), both writing in the US context.

identities became exaggerated during this era and, even though these notions have never fully reflected actual life situations of many men and women, with many poor women always participating in paid work, for example, these assumptions were exported to many societies through colonial processes.[4] These assumptions continue to influence many government policies and remain powerful influences in many workplaces, communities and families across different societies today.[5]

Yet a number of social and economic forces have arisen as potential challenges to these assumptions. We call these *potential levers for change*. While change over time is inevitable, we focus in this book on change towards more equitable, satisfying and sustainable ways of harmonising paid work with other parts of life, for men as well as for women (see Chapter 3). Various potential levers for change, such as growing numbers of women in paid work, advances in technology, economic developments and ageing populations, have affected different countries at different phases in their social evolutions and have led to different responses and supports for combining different parts of life, with diverse effects. For example, concerns about the welfare of children have kept some mothers out of the labour market at some periods of history in some countries, whereas in other contexts, it has prompted quality nursery provision. However, while many social and economic forces provide potential levers for change, such changes are not always equitable and not always sustained. Very often potential levers simply lead to surface change or quick fixes. These can be seen when labour market inequalities between men and women are addressed by initiatives to increase the sheer numbers of women in senior positions in the workplace without recognising that workplaces and men, as well as women, have to change too.

Below we offer brief evolutionary 'snapshots' of the seven countries to set the context for subsequent chapters. Our snapshots first look back by focusing on social and economic forces that have been potential or actual levers for change over the second half of the twentieth century. We then explore responses of governments and formal workplace organisations. Although other institutions, especially trade unions and NGOs, have also played significant roles in these social evolutions, to a greater or lesser extent, in all the countries, we focus on government and workplaces. We recognise that situations evolve, sometimes slowly, sometimes rapidly, and that there will inevitably be new and potentially significant developments in different contexts. However, each snapshot attempts to reflect current situations in different countries at the time of writing. We end each snapshot by beginning to look forward by discussing emerging forces that may become potential levers for change in the future. Sometime these forces, such as population ageing or HIV/AIDS,

---

[3] This tied in with Victorian ideology about 'separate spheres' for men and women. However, as Jane Lewis and David Piachaud (1987) highlight in a historical account of the women's experience of poverty in the UK, poor women have always had to work. Yet trade union demanded protective legislation curbing the hours that women and children could work further cemented women's marginal position in the labour market and increased their vulnerability to poverty.

[4] We have already alluded in the last footnote that poor women have always had to work. But women who remained unmarried were also expected to be active in paid employment although often in professions 'suitable' for their characteristics and abilities. Megan Doolittle (2004) offers an interesting account of unmarried women's labour market participation during the two world wars. Using a blend of feminist and Kleinian psychoanalytic perspectives, she discusses the ways in which some of these women were encouraged to sublimate and split off their own maternal feelings and project these into nanny and governess employment. John Tosh (1999) also offers insights into men's changing involvement in the home during the Victorian era. In particular, he observes that the fathers' involvement in the education and guidance of their sons was important. For a lucid discussion of the ways in which stereotypical notions of femininity and masculinity, or women's work and men's work were exported to some non-western countries and cultures through colonial processes see Connell (2004).

[5] These assumptions continue to be exported to non-western societies today through contemporary globalisation processes (see Rapoport et al., 2002), as well as neocolonial processes (see Said, 1993 and Chakrabarty, 2000 for more general accounts).

are seen as crises. Yet these very challenges can bring societies to a turning point and may become levers for more equitable, satisfying and sustainable change in the future.

INDIA

Looking Backwards: Potential Levers for Change

Although women in India have always worked in the informal economy, especially in rural areas, the formal labour force participation of women from a range of backgrounds has increased in recent decades.[6] The impact of women's employment on expectations and assumptions about men and women's roles and relationships however, has been limited (Ramu, 1987). This is partly because domestic servants in middle-class families, and the availability of members of extended families more generally in the population, have somewhat cushioned the 'work–family' conflicts and tensions that could lead to change (Sekaran, 1992).

A more significant force for change was the opening of the economy in 1991. This brought more exposure to global competitiveness and opportunities to develop economically. The spread of multinationals and the emergence of India as an IT outsourcing destination brought material gains, rising wages, better employment prospects and consumer choices for a growing minority. However, our participants note that the increasingly demanding workloads and long working hours make it more difficult for those working in the new economy to harmonise paid work with other parts of life.

Other potential levers for further change have included shifts in family structures and growing challenges in the care of the elderly. Extended families, which have traditionally provided substantial support for childcare and other care have begun to give way to nuclear families in more affluent circles, linked in part to urbanisation trends and rising costs of housing.[7] Many poorer families also experience the separation of joint families as certain family members migrate in search of paid work. In this shifting context, as the population ages, care of the elderly is creating specific pressures for some families.

Government Responses

Some government policy measures emerged early on to support women in formal employment. In the late 1940s, limits were put on working hours and workplaces were required to provide crèches if they employed more than 30 women on a full-time basis. However, some employers got round this by extending temporary contracts for women, and many employers we met were not aware of legal crèche obligations. Entitlements to 12 weeks paid maternity leave were also introduced in the early 1960s,[8] and legislation on equal pay

---

[6] The numbers of women in formal paid work in both urban and rural areas rose during the 1970s and accelerated greatly during the 1980s (Raju & Bagchi, 1993). Women from middle and upper middle class backgrounds also began to enter paid work for the first time during this period, with motivations ranging from economic to self-fulfillment (Rani, 1976). However, assumptions that 'ideal' mothers are those who spend time focusing on nurturing their children remain strong barriers amongst many women. During the 1970s and 1980s, women's studies and research on affluent as well as less privileged women also became an area of research in some major universities. Some of this research touched on 'work–family' dilemmas and gender issues. At the same time, research on work–family relations in urban settings also appeared. Yet research has not explored organisational levels and connections. See Rajdhyahsha and Smita (2004) for a more detailed account.
[7] See Sekaran (1984) for an early study documenting this trend.

and equal treatment for men and women emerged in the 1970s, although as elsewhere, a pay gap between men and women continues.[9] Overall there is limited legislative or state welfare support for harmonising paid work with other parts of life, and limited social security more generally. The liberalisation of the economy has further encouraged market solutions and reductions in the role of the state (Poster, 2005).

Workplaces

Some large formal organisations, particularly those exposed to global quality standards, are beginning to introduce policies and procedures to recruit, retain and support employees. 'Work–life balance' terminology has caught on in the context of the pressures of long working hours and intensity of work and 'work–life balance' was identified as the number one concern in an employee survey at one large multinational subsidiary located in India. Employer initiatives tend to be geared towards making it easier for employees to spend as much time as possible in paid work. For example, some new economy businesses have brought in stress counselling, concierge services or on-site recreational and social activities.

The increasing demands and pace of work are not limited to professionals or private-sector multinationals. Factory workers are expected to increase their productivity with fewer employees, and public-sector workers also experience much organisational change. Some public-sector organisations have long had 'paternalistic' policies in place: workers are regarded as members of their employers' extended families and there are measures to support the well-being of employees and their families, such as help with housing or workplace-led family based activities. Some Indian private-sector companies have also developed family related policies that tend to comprise material or other benefits to support employees and their families, often negotiated via unions. In a country with little infrastructure or government support, these policies are very important. Yet we hear concern about the extent to which these negotiations will continue. The growth of global competition, drives to cut costs and organisational restructuring have weakened the power of the unions, and led to reductions in many of these policies and approaches (Poster, 2005).

Looking Forwards: Potential Levers for Change?

We hear there has been limited general change in men's behaviour in the home or the workplace, although some individual men are changing. The availability of domestic workers to some extent sustains the status quo among relatively affluent families. It also cushions the effects of any decline in joint families by enabling people to work long hours without having to think about changing work practices, and without changing male and female roles and relationships in the home (Sekaran, 1992). For poorer families there is no support beyond the extended family.

There is concern about the effects of workplace changes – including long working hours and workplace intensity, particularly in new economy jobs, as well as a growth in temporary contracts – on opportunities for people to build relationships in the workplace.

---

[8] The Factories Act 1948 limited working hours and required workplaces to provide crèches if more than 30 women were employed full-time. The Maternity Benefit Act 1961 stipulated that workplaces had to give women short breaks for breastfeeding.

[9] Again, see Rajdhyahsha and Smita (2004) for more detailed information of these developments and impacts.

There is also concern about the lack of time and energy people have to maintain relationships beyond the workplace, or to iron out emerging conflicts between different generations or marital partners. Among many of our participants, especially those working in
the new economy, there is widespread concern about time pressures and the intrusion of
paid work into all areas of life.

> 'There used to be an imbalance towards the life side . . . the change has been positive
> from the consumer point of view . . . but there has been a reverse with an imbalance
> towards the work side and this can cause problems in families' (Indian man, HR
> manager).

However, discussions of 'work–life balance' tend to focus on a tiny percentage of workers
in the new economy, even though issues about harmonising work with other parts of life
affect others such as domestic or rural workers.

There was a widely voiced view among our participants that concerns about harmonising paid work with other parts of life is a luxury that India cannot afford to focus on until
after it has caught up with or exceeded the West in terms of economic development and
competitiveness. Arguably India is in a unique position with its newly gained technological strengths and the potential to learn from the mistakes of 'developed' countries about
what current working practices are doing to people's lives. There has been some recent
media debate about the human, social and cultural costs of the infiltration of foreign companies and associated working practices, and some business leaders have spoken out about
the need for socially sustainable work that accounts for and values other parts of people's
lives, be it family or community involvement. Yet many of our participants feel that the
huge problems India faces, including widespread poverty and lack of infrastructure and
supports, leaves no alternative but to adhere to the dominant model of capitalism that puts
profits first before considering social and personal needs of workers, often experienced as
clashing with India's cultural heritage.

> Indian Society is in a state of flux . . . society is basically at cross roads . . . [We] are
> basically faced with this globalisation, by this challenge that is coming in from the
> West . . . at the same time, we are very much in conflict with our heritage, our beliefs,
> and the kind of mental baggage that has come down to us . . .' (Indian woman,
> government official)

There is talk about the emerging stronger India, which, along with China, will become
one of the biggest economies of the future world. There is some excitement about this but
also concern about what this will do to people.

> 'I fervently hope that as we move forward we will be able to pull it off all together
> with respect and basic dignities of all our people intact' (Indian man, manager).

It remains to be seen whether these pressures – and emerging voices of concern about the
impact of current ways of working – will act as major levers for change.

SOUTH AFRICA

Looking Backwards: Potential Levers for Change

As in India, many women in South Africa have always worked in the informal economy,
but women's participation in the formal labour market has grown in recent decades
(Barker, 2003). However, the potential of this trend to drive change in workplaces and

families has been partly obscured by struggles against the injustices of apartheid. Given the focus on racial inequalities, our participants feel that equity between men and women and issues of harmonising paid work with other parts of life have received much less attention.[10]

> 'Race is very important given our history. Gender is too, but I guess we haven't really got to that stage yet' (South African woman, HR manager).

Nevertheless, our participants point out that the new post-apartheid Constitution emphasises general equality principles which helps to drive change.

Other important potential drivers of change have been economic developments, especially the reintegration of South Africa into the global economy after the post-apartheid transformation to a democracy in 1994, and pressures to overcome widespread poverty and income inequalities. Trade liberalisation and exposure to the global economy has brought intensive international competition and strong internal and external pressures to enhance productivity and efficiency. This often results in employees feeling overworked.

Other potential levers include a 'brain drain' as many white people leave the country – usually attributed to persisting racial tensions. There is therefore concern amongst many organisations about how to support and retain skilled employees, and this is beginning to prompt government and employers to think about a range of measures to enhance employees' experiences at work. This has the potential to spread to initiatives for harmonising paid work with other parts of life in more optimal ways.

The spread of HIV/AIDS is also emerging as a major force for change, challenging employers to rethink many working practices. One of our participants, who works with AIDS sufferers, argued that the spread of HIV/AIDS may be a lever for change in relation to men and women's roles and relationships because there is widespread acknowledgement that AIDS is a disease that affects men and women in different ways.[11] Women are much more biologically vulnerable to infection and also tend to have more responsibility for caring for those affected by the virus, which also impacts on their paid working lives.

Government Responses

Some government policies are in place to assist people in harmonising paid work with other parts of life, including paid maternity leave, limited paid parental leave and sickness and compassionate leave particularly in light of AIDS related illnesses and death. However, these policies are only available to those in formal work. As the formal unemployment rate is so high in South Africa, many people engaged in informal work slip through the net.[12]

---

[10] Among our participants, black women we spoke with said their voices were largely silenced as they were discouraged from 'diluting' the struggle against apartheid by raising gender issues. At the same time, many white women were actively researching and advocating greater gender equity. There have also been pockets of innovations such as gender awareness training for black and white women and men, facilitated by Rhona Rapoport and others in the early 1990s. Yet our participants agree that equity between men and women has received less attention than race equity.

[11] Women and men are driven by social constructions of their gender to play out roles such as 'passive woman' or 'risk taking men'. The World Health Organisation (http://www.who.int/gender/hiv_aids/en/) documents this problem and the connections with HIV/AIDS infections.

[12] The official employment rate stood at 27.8 per cent in 2004 (Statistics South Africa, 2004, http://www.statssa.gov.za/news_archive/news_archive.asp), although there is much agreement that it is probably over 40 per cent.

The post-apartheid Constitution includes legislation requiring workplace organisations to have employment-equity forums bringing together employers, employees and trade unions to discuss many types of equity issues in the workplace. There are also affirmative action programmes to increase the numbers of black people, including all non-white ethnic groups, other ethnicities and women in more senior positions. The Government has shown a willingness to intervene at the workplace level to support productivity drives, for example, funding initiatives to enhance performance through innovative worker participation projects (Maree & Godfrey, 2003). All this reflects potential to extend workplace forums and participative projects to issues about harmonising paid work with other parts of life. At the moment, however, these challenges are only just beginning to be discussed, even though a general absence of 'work–family' supports has been noted, making it particularly difficult for people to combine the different parts of life.[13]

Workplaces

There are pockets of discussions in workplaces about harmonising work with other parts of life in workplaces, but these are mainly confined to large companies, especially multinationals. Equity concerns are discussed, but many of our participants say that affirmative action policies to increase the numbers of women as well as black people in paid work have not moved beyond boosting numbers.

Nevertheless there is some evidence that change might come about at the workplace level as a response to the HIV/AIDS epidemic. This poses many challenges for employers who will have to adapt to the potential loss of up to one-third of employees countrywide who will die of the virus. Participants report that workplaces are starting to look into ways in which they can enable people at later stages of infection to sustain employment by providing shorter working hours and extending sick leaves. Some workplaces are also engaged in prevention initiatives, including advice about condom use. However, although we heard of extensions in compassionate leaves to attend funerals, there have been fewer developments in terms of enabling carers of people with AIDS to change their working practices – thus exacerbating risks of poverty for carers and their families.[14]

Looking Forwards: Potential Levers for Change?

There is no national debate about the harmonisation of paid work with other parts of life. Instead, there is an understandable pre-occupation with many other major societal problems and issues, namely HIV/AIDS, unemployment, crime and poverty. While the men and women with whom we talked discussed current difficulties in harmonising paid work with other parts of life, they told us that these issues are not widely articulated. As in India, we hear that in the context of a need to 'develop' more areas of the country, many workers accept long working hours and intensive working practices. They feel 'there is no altern-

---

[13] See Aryee (2005), who discusses work–family challenges in Sub-Saharan Africa noting the problems and paucity of research in this area.

[14] There are very small government allowances for people at later stages of AIDS infection, but this does not extend to carers. There are also child support grants, which can help families who have lost the main breadwinner through AIDS or because of unemployment. But these are means tested and, again, reflect very low amounts (see Van Niekerk, 2003).

ative' despite the impact that these working practices have on time for family care and other parts of life. Nevertheless, high levels of unemployment alongside growing workplace intensity and long hours for those who are employed are causing some people to ask whether or not trends for downsizing to compete in the global economy are ethical. This was a major question that arose and stimulated heated discussion in the country meeting.

South Africans are aware that policies, while important for cementing rights, are not enough for optimal change. The influential approach and guidance of Nelson Mandela, has sensitised South Africans to the need for an ongoing process approach to work through deeply embedded inequities and identity issues at multiple levels of society.

> 'People in South Africa are aware of the need to go through processes . . . we had so much healing to do in terms of race, and that was a long process . . . something that is still going on' (South African woman, academic).

However, processes of change involve working with resistance and in South Africa this includes an emerging backlash against black economic empowerment initiatives,[15] affirmative action and equity forums from white men in particular who feel threatened by these. Some employers are also concerned that equity and affirmative action initiatives may impact on competitiveness in the global economy.

Despite the recognition of the importance of a processes focused approach, this has not yet been widely considered in relation to the goal of equity between men and women or problems associated with combining paid work with other parts of life. Nevertheless, lessons learned about the processes of social change and the challenges presented by other social problems such as the effects of HIV/AIDS may provide seeds that could germinate when challenges about harmonising the many parts of life are taken on board.

JAPAN

Looking Backwards: Potential Levers for Change

Although 'traditional' assumptions about men and women's roles are particularly embedded in Japanese culture, the numbers of women in formal paid work rose dramatically during the 1980s.[16] About 50 per cent of all women are now in formal paid work: a figure which has remained relatively constant since the 1990s.[17] However, long working hours and other expectations can make it difficult for women with caring responsibilities to participate in many jobs that men do. Although many women say they would like to remain active in the labour market during the child rearing period (Gender Equality Bureau, 2004), most mothers leave paid work when their children are born and return on a part-time basis when their children are a little older. This contributes to the high earnings gap between men and women: a gap that exists to some extent in all the countries. The difficulties that

---

[15] Black economic empowerment is an initiative through which black people are encouraged to achieve power through ownership of capital and business. One of our participants discussed empowerment deals that have the potential to change power relations in the country. However, at the same time, as noted by Frogett (2002), writing more generally in the UK context, there is a danger that initiatives such as these can lead to competition and resentment rather than recognition and empowerment.

[16] Before the Second World War, many women worked outside of the home, but rapid economic growth and increasing financial security meant many were able to 'choose' to be full-time housewives from the 1950s onwards. However, subsequent economic downturns, combined with changing aspirations of women, have all contributed to the rise in women's formal paid work participation.

[17] For examination and explanation about the past and contemporary patterns of women's labour market participation, see www.jiwe.or.jp/english/evolusion/index.html (please note, a misspelling of evolution is in the website address).

women experience in combining demanding employment expectations with family life, also contribute to a declining birth rate, which currently stands well below replacement levels. This is a major concern in Japan and a particular potential lever for change.

Population ageing, linked to declining fertility but also greater longevity, is also a potential lever for change. Elder care was identified as a concern earlier than in many other countries. Women take on much of the responsibilities for caring for older parents and parents-in-law and are often penalised in workplaces as a result (Chabot, 1992). The government has recently introduced long-term care insurance, so that the elderly will be able to 'buy in' required care, but there is much discussion about the long-term financial sustainability of this as the population continues to age. Workplaces may need to adapt more to enable older people to work longer and to enable carers of older people to combine employment with family responsibilities.

Government Responses

In response to demographic concerns a National Commission on the Falling Birth Rate was set up to examine how to better support men and women in combining paid work with their family responsibilities. Emerging policies to address these challenges focus on paid leave arrangements for parents during the early years and when children are sick. Maternity leave has long been available and there are now more recent parental leave entitlements, although the take-up by men is very low.[18] There are also statutory entitlements for time to care for elderly relatives.

In 1999, the Government declared its commitment to equal opportunities to participate in employment and family life for men and women and has set targets to get more women in senior positions in workplaces. The Government has recently funded research on how to encourage more men to take parental leave and has also introduced awards for the most 'family-friendly' companies to encourage the spread of 'good practice'. The terminology used to discuss combining paid work with other parts of life, like the use of employer awards, is very much influenced by the West, especially the USA. However, 'family-friendly' practices have not spread widely.

Workplaces

A very 'masculine' ethos prevails in Japanese workplaces, and this excludes many women especially those with family responsibilities in a number of ways. For example, there is a history of long working hours, exacerbated by long commutes and traditions of work-related evening socialising. However, there are signs that this may be changing: one of our participants says commutes are becoming shorter as house prices in cities are falling and work-related evening socialising is declining because of individual economic pressures.

In the context of intensive working practices, initiatives to address people's family needs include 'family-friendly' policies, such as cafeteria benefits that offer a menu of benefits adapted from US companies. Participants tell us that 'family-friendly' policies are increasingly defined as 'work–life compatible' policies, which may indicate greater inclusion of men and others without direct family responsibilities as well as potential connections

---

[18] In 1999 only 2.4 per cent of all people who took parental leave were men (Iwao, 2003). See http://www.daiwa-foundation.org.uk/_pdf/Iwao%20transcript.pdf.

with a business case for change. But the focus on policies without process oriented change leaves core values and assumptions untouched. In some companies distinctions are made between 'family-friendly' policies and other types of 'work-life compatible' policies, such as flexi-time. 'Family-friendly' policies, such as opportunities to take leave or work part-time, are taken mostly by women, who are often marginalised for using them, whereas other innovations such as flexi-time are largely seen as productivity measures so these are taken up by men as well as women. This illustrates a generic finding across the countries; that policies directed at women or families are often marginalised while those perceived to be productivity measures are more likely to be brought into the mainstream.

Looking Forwards: Potential Levers for Change?

Concerns about the birth rate and care of the elderly remain strong. Our participants also voiced concerns about the impact of intense workplace demands on couple relationships. There is talk of less time to form or maintain personal relationships and a divorce rate that has steadily risen since the 1960s.

Long and intensive working hours make it difficult for women with caring responsibil-ities to advance in workplaces and make it difficult for men to become more involved in family life.

> 'Younger men want to be with their family members but they feel the everyday needs of the workplace hold them back' (Japan, government advisor).

Recent incorporation of 'work-life balance' or 'work-life compatible' terminology reflects growing concern about long hours and the growing demands of intensification of work. An interesting development has been requests for shorter hours instead of wage rises by some male dominated unions in their 2004 annual bargaining negotiations. This has gen-erated some optimism.

> 'This period of economic instability has meant people are asking whether there might be other things that are more important than money' (Japanese man, manager).

Thus, there are some seeds of change with indications of an emerging tendency towards small reductions in working hours amongst men and women in full-time employment. However, economic instability is a double-edged sword: participants tell us that many people are afraid to take up entitlements to family leaves or flexibility for fear they may be seen as less committed, more costly to companies and thus more likely to lose their jobs. In this context, people close to government recognise that policies alone are not working, and attention is beginning to shift to workplace cultures and practices. There is some optimism about this, but many concede Japanese men's identity is strongly linked to their paid work and widespread change will be not be easy.

USA

Looking Backwards: Potential Levers for Change

In the USA, the major potential lever for change has been the increasing female labour force participation. This is due to economic necessity in many cases as two incomes are increasingly needed to survive or to maintain particular standards of living but it has also been influenced by feminist demands and reactions against idealisations of the housewife role.[19] Employers also made efforts to attract and retain women's labour as the economy flourished.[20] Interest in men as fathers needing time with their families also emerged from the 1970s onwards (Levine & Pittinsky, 1997; Pleck & Masciadrelli, 2003).

Paradoxically, lack of state support for harmonising paid work and the rest of life has served as a lever for change in some respects, as it has encouraged corporations to take notice of problems in combining paid work with other parts of life, at least for more skilled and valued employees.[21] However, more recently, massive and rapid changes in the nature of paid work in the global market have occurred, which can jeopardise the potential success of many employer initiatives.

Government Responses

Legislative measures securing women's equal rights began in the late 1960s and affirmative action within the workplace was developed during the 1970s. However, there was limited success in linking this with government support for harmonising paid work with family life, either by regulating employers or through supporting childcare.[22] Combining paid work with family and personal life was and continues to be regarded largely as an individual responsibility and of no concern of the Federal Government or individual states (although there is much state variation). Our participants confirmed that many people in the USA do not expect much support from the Government and have little or no sense of entitlement to associated measures and initiatives.[23]

The USA is one of very few countries in the world where there is no universal entitlement to paid maternity leave (Gornick & Meyers, 2003; Heymann, Earle & Hanchate, 2004). The Family and Medical Leave Act was finally passed in 1993 to give some carers the right to take time out of the labour market, but this leave is unpaid and small employers are exempt so it is not available to all employees. The first large-scale bill funding childcare was passed in 1990 but childcare support remains very minimal.

Lack of a national health service also means many people gain health and medical insurance through work-related benefits, thus increasing people's dependence on employers and there is little in the way of a social safety net for those who are not in paid work. The employment rate in the USA is very high, but with little regulation many jobs are poorly paid with few benefits and often with irregular and unpredictable hours (see Henly &

---

[19] The women's liberation movement was particularly forceful in the USA, influenced by early books such as *The Feminine Mystique* (Friedan, 1963), and other cultural forces.

[20] For a more detailed account of US evolutions of work–personal life issues, see the timeline and accompanying essay by Pruitt and Rapoport (2003).

[21] See Den Dulk (2005), who found that a lack of public provisions for reconciling paid work and family prompts more organisational measures, but that these organisational measures are characterised by inequality of coverage and access. Writing about the situation in the USA in comparative perspective, Gornick and Meyers (2003, p. 8) note that: 'The United States does far less than many similarly rich countries to redistribute and equalize income or to actively manage labour markets. We also do much less to socialize the costs of care-giving – through government policies that redistribute income to families with children, public services that reduce employment penalties associated with devoting time to care-giving, or labour market regulations that protect parents' time with their children.' In their exhaustative study, the authors demonstrate that this has particular implications for families experiencing poverty, including low earning couples and lone mother households who receive less public support to enable them to reconcile paid work with care responsibilities. This is made worse in the context of a low-wage economy in which they have very few resources to buy in support services and can struggle to make ends meet even when in full-time work. See also Lambert (1999) on the challenges confronting low wage workers in combining work and family in the USA.

[22] This is despite the efforts of pioneers such as Congresswoman Pat Schroeder.

[23] Several US polls also suggest that Americans tend to distrust government sponsored programmes.

Lambert, 2004). There is also a lack of protection for part-time workers who are not covered by the Federal Labor Standards Act, the core US labour law.

Workplaces

In the absence of public support for childcare and statutory entitlements to family leaves, companies experienced pressures from employees, prominent NGOs and research organisations such as the Families and Work Institute, some unions and some advocates to introduce what became known as 'family-friendly' policies – a term that soon caught on in the UK and other countries. Significant workplace initiatives developed in some companies including various forms of dependent care supports and alternative working arrangements. However, these are often only at the policy level and predominantly in larger organisations (some of whom recognize the need to go beyond policy to, for example, train supervisors), and although some smaller organisations have informal flexibility and support, many employees, including the most vulnerable, are not covered. While such policies are necessary they are not sufficient and tend to leave mainstream structures, cultures and practices largely untouched.

An interesting development has been the emergence of a 'work–life' profession including external consultants offering support and advice on work–family issues such as childcare, and 'work–life managers' employed internally within human resources departments of large organisations. For some external consultants this became a thriving business – a market response to an issue created by the market capitalist system. However, while the work–family specialists with whom we spoke feel that they have been important in raising the visibility of work and family matters in workplaces, other participants argue that the location of most work–family managers within HR departments as well as current trends to outsource HR have served to marginalise these concerns. Many 'work–life' professionals lack strategic influence, and the policies and initiatives that they develop tend to be individualistic rather than changing wider workplace systems.[24] Consequently, many employees are reluctant to make use of 'family-friendly' or 'work–life' initiatives for fear they might jeopardise their career prospects or job security.[25]

There are also annual awards for the most 'family-friendly' companies (as there are in Japan and the UK), organised by private institutions such as *Working Mothers* magazine.[26] These tend to be highly visible in the USA and some employers strive to be on lists exemplifying their 'good practice'. However, there is growing awareness that even when 'family-friendly' policies exist they are often targeted at women[27] and they are not enough

---

[24] One of our participants talked of a growing divide between work–family professionals, who often tend to see the solution in terms of policies, and the many researchers who point to the limitation of policies and the need to ask bigger questions and seek more fundamental changes. She talked about these two groups 'climbing separate mountains'.

[25] See Hochschild (1997) and Albrecht (2003) who document the lack of take-up of 'work–life' initiatives by those interested in workplace advancement.

[26] There has also been a recent Work-Life Legacy Award developed by the Families and Work Institute that pays tribute to people who have been particularly influential in research, policy and practice developments. Of particular significance is the new Alfred P. Sloan Award for Business Excellence in Workplace Flexibility, lead by the Families and Work Institute, the Center for Workplace Preparation, an affiliate of the US Chamber of Commerce, and the Twiga Foundation. It will be given in 24 communities by 2007 and, importantly, two-thirds of the points for winners come from a survey of employees in those organisations.

[27] The Families and Work Institute National Study of Employers 2005 indicates that many large employers are beginning to understand the importance of moving beyond policy and taking a life-course approach for equity and backlash reasons and from employee surveys. The 2002 national Study of the Changing Workforce shows that the biggest changes in recent years have been among men – especially younger men – a trend also evident in the UK; see, for example, O'Brien & Shemilt (2003).

to make a difference. Research indicates that informal support from managers and colleagues is more significant (Allen, 2001; Thompson, 1999).

Our participants stressed that the contradictions between prevailing workplace cultures and formal policies and programmes are a major concern. More and more women share the breadwinning role, and men have an increasing share of some child and other care responsibilities, but assumptions about 'ideal' workers as those able to put the job first no matter what, remain firmly entrenched in most workplaces.[28] Moreover, employers' interest in 'work–family' or 'work–life' policies have developed alongside other employer trends, such as downsizing and efficiency drives, designed to encourage employees to work more intensively. Consequently women face major time pressures, as do growing numbers of men, and heavy care responsibilities can reinforce inequities between men and women, just as the lack of government support and reliance on employers reinforces inequities between high and low skilled workers.

Looking Forwards: Current Concerns and Emerging Potential Levers for Change?

There is growing awareness that issues about harmonising paid work with family and personal life affect both men and women, and that personal life needs are not restricted to childcare. In the USA, as elsewhere, care of the elderly is causing increasing pressures and concerns for many families[29].

Our participants talk about a culture of 'overwork', blurred boundaries between work and other parts of life due to high work demands, and technological developments that keep people constantly 'on-message'. Some higher earning families cope with heavy demands by employing domestic help. However, many problems persist, particularly for women and those on lower incomes with caring commitments, who are not able to pay for domestic and care support and often have unpredictable jobs that make childcare difficult to arrange (see Henly & Lambert, 2004). Intensive workplace cultures and current ways of working, combined with a lack of childcare facilities, has prompted growing concern about crises of care and the impact this has on families and communities.[30]

In this context, small pockets of innovative practice have emerged, including action-orientated research within some leading-edge companies that seeks to change workplace structures, cultures and practices.[31] But these approaches, which we discuss in more detail in Chapter 3, take time and do not hold out the promise of the quick fixes that so many employers seek.

Though there is growing interest in redefining work, in general, responses have focused on individual responsibility and individual options rather than seeing these issues as collective or state concerns. Moreover one of our co-researchers told us that the global

---

[28] This makes work–family challenges difficult for lone mothers particularly given expectations to participate in paid work without corresponding childcare supports and provisions (see Ferguson, 2004, for a discussion of welfare to work schemes in both the UK and the USA).

[29] New York Times (2005): an article by Jane Gross, November 24th, discusses one woman's decision to forget her career to look after her elderly parents. Yet the question of men potentially giving up their careers, or the potential of rethinking workplace practices, are not raised.

[30] See Harrington (1999) and Heilbrun, Heston and Weiner (1999) for full discussions. See also Ehrenreich and Hochschild (2003) for an exploration of the reasons for and discussion of the impact of the increasing use of migrant labour to make up for care shortfalls. In terms of the impact on communities, see Putnam (2000) and Bookman (2004).

[31] Examples include work done by: Rapoport, Bailyn, Kolb and Fletcher, 1996; Rapoport, Bailyn, Fletcher and Pruitt, 2002; Bailyn and Harrington, 2004. Alongside this, small pockets of action research in families have also emerged, which seeks to work with men and women by challenging assumptions of 'ideal' mothers and fathers (see Degroot & Fine, 2003).

economy and its pressures have upped the ante and change will be even harder to achieve in this economic climate. All this perpetuates major inequalities between rich and poor, and advantaged and disadvantaged in this richest of countries. Nevertheless, current working structures, cultures and practices that continue to cause so many difficulties for harmonising work with other parts of life are being exported to many other countries, particularly with the outsourcing of work to countries where labour costs are cheaper and where multinational organisations operate.

SOME EUROPEAN EXAMPLES

Countries in Europe provide models of socio-economic development in which the importance of government actions are emphasised, albeit to varying degrees. Many welfare states in Europe are founded on the basis of *social* citizenship or entitlements, with rights to education, health and social security traditionally justified as necessary for social and economic well-being. Compared to Americans, Europeans enjoy more employment protection, more support if they are unemployed, and more public support for child or elder care responsibilities.

Although there have been cuts in public spending in many European countries in recent years, these principles and supports remain. Yet there are many different forms of welfare states or 'regimes' within Europe.[32] Below we discuss our findings in the three European countries we have included in our study. The UK, closest to the USA, is often classified as a 'liberal' welfare state, as it puts more emphasis on the market and except for services such as education and health, often sees the state as a last point of call. Adoption of work–family initiatives tend to be framed in terms of a business case with an emphasis on benefits for organisations. The welfare state in The Netherlands is particularly difficult to classify, but in terms of work–family or work–personal life challenges, it has until recently actively supported 'traditional' roles for men and women. In this context, it reflects a 'conservative' welfare state in which the role of the family is emphasised and external care provisions are limited (Den Dulk, 2005). Norway is classified as a 'social democratic' welfare state because of its widespread use of universal provisions and its extensive development of services, including childcare, that have emphasis on supporting female labour market participation.[33]

Government policies in the UK and The Netherlands have both been influenced by the European Union, which plays an important role in relation to the reconciliation of family and employment in member states.[34] Directives, including those on parental leave and rights for part-time workers, which must be implemented by member state governments,

---

[32] Of course welfare typologies also refer to welfare states or regimes beyond Europe, such as particular arrangements in the USA, Japan and Australasia. See Esping-Andersen (1990) for an extremely influential, albeit criticised, typology of welfare states in many contemporary 'developed' societies. As well as criticisms on the extent to which countries fit the types he puts them into, or the extent to which classification can change over time, a major criticism of Esping-Andersen has been his failure to fully consider how different welfare states treat women. See Lewis (1992) and Sainsbury (1994) for more gender-sensitive discussions. Jane Lewis (1992) suggests categorising countries by the extent to which they operate a weak, modified or strong male breadwinner arrangement. Orloff (1993) suggests using Esping-Andersen's typologies but extending these to explore the extent to which women can form autonomous households and the extent to which women are supported to participate in paid work alongside care responsibilities. For more discussion of welfare regimes in 'developing' countries, see Gough and Wood (2004).

[33] It is often argued that Norway has historically placed less of an emphasis on women's labour market participation than other Scandinavian countries, such as Sweden. Yet positions have now more or less converged (see Leira, 1992).

[34] Norway is not a member of the EU, but already has more or equally progressive regulation on reconciliation of family and employment than various EU states.

are negotiated at the European level by employee, employer and government representatives (known as the social partners), in a process of 'social dialogue'.

THE UK

Looking Backwards: Potential Levers for Change

Although British women, particularly poorer women, have always participated in paid work as a matter of financial necessity, assumptions about women's primary association with family care have been strong in recent history. These assumptions were particularly ingrained during the 1950s, following influential but contested work by John Bowlby and others on the importance of the mother–child relationship for child development.[35] Yet the frustrations many housewives felt during this period were documented in some academic and popular books,[36] resulting in much feminist campaigning in the late 1960s and 1970s. This, combined with growing needs of employers for female labour market participation,[37] led to a subsequent rise of women from all walks of life entering formal paid work particularly from the 1980s onwards. This has been an important potential lever for change.

However, in the context of a lack of public provisions and support for childcare and other types of care, many women, particularly mothers with young children, work in short hours, part-time jobs, often in low status positions as promotion can require full-time and long hours of work. This contributes to gaps in pay between men and women. Meanwhile, British men (and women employed full-time) work the longest hours in Europe, which has further spurred attention to 'work–life balance' challenges.

Other potential levers for change have included the growth in the number of lone mothers and Government dilemmas about whether to support them as mothers or workers in the context of drives to curb public expenditure. The European Union with its agenda to support men and women to reconcile employment with family life has also been a major lever for change.

Government Responses

Legislation for equal pay, outlawing of sex discrimination, and entitlements to paid maternity leave were introduced in the 1970s. However, in recent history, successive governments were reluctant to implement policies, such as publicly provided childcare, to support men and women to combine paid work with family life in equitable ways. Moreover, many welfare policies and benefits have encouraged male breadwinner and female carer roles.[38]

---

[35] See Bowlby (1953), Winnicott (1968) and Douglas and Michaels (2004) for a recent synthesis and critique of these accounts.

[36] See Simone de Beauvoir (1953), whose book, *The Second Sex*, was published in English and included the observation that it was difficult to reconcile work and maternity under current conditions. Many women in the UK, as in the USA, were influenced by Friedan (1963), realising that they were not alone in feeling unfulfilled by home and family responsibilities. See also Hannah Gavron (1966), Rapoport and Rapoport (1965), Rapoport and Rapoport (1971) and Mitchell (1966), which were also forerunners of a reconceptualisation of work and family issues.

[37] See Fogarty, Rapoport and Rapoport (1971), whose work was commissioned by the Leverhulme Foundation following findings from the Robbins Commission on the need for more women in paid work.

[38] The idea of male breadwinners and women as dependent family carers has been written into much post-war social policy and benefit entitlements. See Lister (1994) and (2003) for examples of the vast literature in this area.

However, there have been dramatic shifts in government approaches in recent years, driven by EU Directives, economic concerns and a pledge to eradicate child poverty. There has been a steady stream of initiatives to support lone mothers and mothers in low income households into paid work since the election of New Labour in 1997,[39] alongside attempts to stimulate affordable childcare and enhancements of maternity leave.[40] Recent emphasis has also been placed on the importance of father care involvement, with measures such as the introduction of two weeks' paid paternity leave and unpaid parental leave. There are now rights for parents with children under six to ask for flexible working, although this can be refused on 'business grounds'. Working time legislation with a maximum of 48 hours a week has also been introduced. Currently this comes with an opt-out clause to which employees are often expected to sign up, although the legality of this is being challenged by the EU.

The Government's approach seeks to encourage employers into voluntary action, as the market permits, rather than to regulate for change. They are adopting a two-pronged approach: building a statutory minimum framework of rights in relation to 'work–life balance' while encouraging employers to go further to enhance productivity and competitiveness. The 'business case' for change, promoted by the current Government, encourages many workplace organisations to think about new ways to work, and a wealth of 'best' practice case studies as examples and guidelines have been published by the Department of Trade and Industry. The Government has also allocated funding for consultants to go into organisations (the Challenge Fund) to help workplaces bring about changes in the ways that employees can balance paid work with family and personal life. This has the potential to move employers on beyond policy to practice and ideally bring about actual change in workplace practices, structures and cultures. However, although an innovative approach, funding has generally been short-term and requires quick reporting of results. More recently, the Government appears to be playing down the 'business case' as it introduces more legislation.

Workplaces

In the context of a recent history of minimal state support, some employers, particularly larger organisations relying substantially on women's labour, began to adapt working practices in the 1980s. This was partly to recruit and retain women employees for business reasons, and partly in response to pressure from women. The focus was on policies and benefits, often adapting practices being introduced in the US, but also breaking new ground with innovations such as career breaks. This trend slowed down in the economic recession of the early 1990s – these policies were widely regarded as costs by employers and many employees were more concerned about job insecurity – but resumed as the economy improved.

---

[39] Low levels of benefits for those not in paid work have always been in place. But New Labour has attempted to make the transition from welfare-to-work more economically attractive and easier for marginalised groups. Welfare-to-work initiatives include the New Deal for lone mothers, the Working Families Tax and Child Care tax credits for low earning families.

[40] In the context of efforts to boost affordable childcare, see Williams (2004), who explores the limitations of current initiatives. In particular she notes (2004, p. 29): 'Most childcare provision is in the private sector, and in spite of financial help, for those not on professional salaries is just too expensive – childcare costs are 25% of the average household income. This may be why only 13% of those eligible to receive financial support for childcare [which has to be spent on registered child minders in order to receive it] had taken up their Childcare Tax Credits in 2002.' On the problems of extending maternity leave, several authors document the problems this can create for women who subsequently lose opportunities to develop their labour market employability, thus in turn further entrenching the immediate viability for men and women to operate a gendered division of labour (see Lister, 2003; Gornick & Meyers, 2003).

However, as elsewhere, it became apparent that policies alone were limited, bringing about some change for women at the margins but not affecting mainstream structures, culture and practices (Lewis, 1997; Lewis, 2001). Workplace norms and assumptions about 'ideal' workers persist, as they do in other countries, perpetuating inequities between men and women. Although there has been much hype about 'work–life balance' initiatives, these tend to be short termist and individualistic. Although there are some notable exceptions, including change programmes undertaken by the Trades Union Congress, advocacy groups and some individual change processes in small organisations,[41] initiatives are rarely strategic and often fail to focus on change in workplace structures, cultures and practices.

Looking Forwards: Potential Levers for Change?

Although 'work–life balance' is now receiving a great deal of attention, much concern remains about Britain's long hours' culture. Organisational trends towards flexible working arrangements have emerged at the same time as increased global competition pressures and the search for ever more 'efficient' ways of working, resulting in what has been described as an intensification of work (see Burchall, Lapido & Wilkinson, 2002). An intensification of work refers to increasing employer expectations in paid work often in the face of downsizing and 'efficiency' drives, as well as changes in work organisation that frequently put more onus on individual responsibility to manage demanding tasks and schedules – a trend that has been noted in all seven countries. Policies are also undermined by the actual or threatened outsourcing of work to cheaper and less regulated countries.

Occupational stress has long been a concern of some employers and employees but is increasingly discussed in terms of not only the workplace, but also in terms of the effects this has on families (Lewis & Cooper, 1999; Sparks, Cooper, Fried, & Shirom, 1997). There is also some concern about population ageing and pensions, resulting in debate about how it may be possible to get people to work longer over the life course.

Government rhetoric stresses the need for employers to consider the needs of men as well as women, but most employers still view 'work–life balance' initiatives as policies for women. Initiatives also remain focused mainly on quick fixes and individual approaches.

In the context of long hours and growing feelings of work-related stress, as well as persisting disparities between the 'work rich' with too much work and the 'work poor' in society (Brannen & Moss, 1998; Hewitt, 1993), discussions are emerging that questions the place and value of paid work in people's lives (Bunting, 2004). Yet, while there is a real feeling that things have come a long way in the UK with government attention and interventions and employer recognition of these issues, participants also talk of their frustrations about a lack of fundamental change.

THE NETHERLANDS

Looking Backwards: Potential Levers for Change

The Netherlands has 'traditionally' been a single breadwinner society with many women excluded from paid employment. Although, in recent decades the number of women in

---

[41] For examples of change processes in small organisations see Lewis and Cooper (2005). Examples of advocacy groups pushing for certain forms and levels of change include Fathers Direct, the Equal Opportunities Commission and the Work Foundation.

paid work has increased dramatically and women's employment rates are now above the European Union average, the vast majority of women work in part-time positions with short hours.[42] As in the UK, the European Union agenda for equal opportunities between men and women including supporting the reconciliation of employment and family life has influenced government agendas and been an important potential lever for change.

Alongside this, the soaring rate of sickness and stress-related early retirements, largely attributed to changes in experiences of paid work, has also acted as a potential lever for change. Our participants talk of prevailing workplace pressures and intensity, and suggest that these have resulted in men and women feeling time and energy pressures, not only in the workplace but also in the home and domestic settings, reflecting some of the connections between the many aspects of life.

Government Responses

The Dutch Government recognises the need for changes in workplaces, families and communities to reflect the increase on women's employment rates. However, although government policy approaches have shifted in recent decades away from supporting single earner families, it has tended to encourage rather than legislate for workplace change. Nevertheless, the Government has provided tax breaks for employers who develop child care facilities, reflecting a public–private partnership. Recent developments also focus on Government and employer funded payments to contribute towards childcare and to be spent on services that parents choose. This reflects a tripartite approach and tries to stimulate responsive provision.[43]

The Government has also funded projects to break down 'traditional' images of masculinity and femininity to try and encourage a shared care approach (Schaapman, 1995),[44] and has set up a Commission to promote and explore innovative changes in adapting from a single breadwinner to a dual-earner model. This includes recognition of the need for change at the workplace level to benefit individuals and business as well as the need to work with communities. With support from the European Union, the Government has also funded a series of experiments within communities and workplaces that seek to change actual working practices and assumptions about how to work.[45]

One exception to the reluctance to legislate is parental leave. In 1991, parental leave was introduced and working parents, both fathers and mothers, were given the right to take six months part-time leave without pay. At that time parental leave could only be taken part-time, supposedly to ensure that employees would keep in touch with their workplace during their time on leave. However, encouraged by the European Union Parental Leave Directive, which sets out minimal conditions but encourages further development, flexible parental leave can be taken on a part- or full-time basis. Parental leave is also paid in the public sector and in some private sector organisations where it is

---

[42] See OECD (2004), which documents that 55 per cent of women aged between 15 and 65 has a job, but that 74 per cent of women work less than 30 hours a week – many with small part-time jobs.

[43] See the Childcare Act, which came into force in January 2005. The Act encourages financial support away from providers towards parents to increase parental choice in terms of provision.

[44] Thanks to Laura Den Dulk for verbal translation.

[45] Some of these initiatives, which aimed to reduce sickness rates have been relatively long term and have focused on a process approach with considerable success (see Van de Bogard, Collins & Van Iren, 2003).

included in collective agreements. This encourages some younger men to work less than full-time, although this tends to be restricted to more educated fathers working in the public sector.[46] Other provisions include, for example, emergency and short-term care leave.

There has been a history of legislation limiting working times to first 48 and then 40 hours a week, which has the potential to mitigate some of the stresses faced in harmonising paid work with the rest of life. However, as in other countries, the growing interest in promoting and enabling flexibility at work, developments in technology and intensified workloads have resulted in many people working more, leading to a blurring of boundaries between paid work and family or other aspects of life.

Workplaces

As elsewhere women's increased employment has been a lever for change in some workplaces, although most adaptation is made by women themselves, for example, working part-time, rather than with wider changes in workplace practices or cultures. 'Work–life' policies are developed unevenly – they are most likely to be developed in large organisations, especially in the public sector or where women's labour is needed (see Remery, Schippers & Van Doorne-Huiskes, 2002[47]). Legislation provides a floor of rights more broadly, but while some men, mainly in the public sector, use parental leave to reduce their working week, the image of the 'ideal' worker as working full-time and not allowing family life to intrude prevails in most organisations. However, the approach to harmonising paid work with other parts of life is not entirely individualistic as flexible working arrangements are increasingly part of collective agreements. Workplace organisations and trade unions are regarded as active participants in developing initiatives.[48] Some workplaces are now developing more innovative approaches, encouraged by the Government's support for bottom–up experiments.

Looking Forwards: Potential Levers for Change?

Rising sickness and disability rates, particularly among women in the 25–40 years age range, continue to be a major concern. One recent response at government level has been to adopt a life course perspective. The Government will shortly implement leaves for everyone, to be taken as required during the life course so as to prevent early burn-out.[49] However, while this recognises people have a diversity of personal life responsibilities that shift across the life course, there has been some concern that this leave will be used by women to manage child and other care responsibilities, while men will use it to take courses to further enhance workplace opportunities or for leisure activities (see Knijn, 2003). Our participants also expressed fears that this might replace parental leave and obscure particular care needs and responsibilities of families or carers. However, it has been noted that given the minimal amounts offered by this leave, it will most likely be

---

[46] The Parental Leave Act (2001) is considered to provide a minimum, which can be supplemented by collective agreements or policies of individual firms, although supplementation is not widespread.

[47] Thanks to Laura Den Dulk for verbal translation.

[48] See Den Dulk (2001), who notes this and indicates that it is becoming an important role for unions.

[49] A life course savings scheme will come into force in 2006.

used by older workers to retire early rather than for parental or leisure leaves earlier in life (see Keuzekamp, 2004[50]).

As in other countries, the ageing population is also a stimulus for Government to enhance opportunities for labour force participation. The problems of harmonising paid work with other parts of life contribute to a trend for women to delay having children: thus some of our participants anticipate future issues relating to the rise of the 'sandwich generation' of families, and women in particular, who may simultaneously experience childcare and care of the elderly commitments.

There continues to be much debate about hours of work and roles of men and women. There was considerable consensus at our country meeting and in the interviews that most women prefer current part-time working patterns and feel that these are best for children. Yet some feel that these assumptions are a legacy of ideas about the importance of the 'ideal' nurturing mother role, combined with a current shortage of full-time childcare pro- vision. At the country meeting, it was noted that media articles continue to evoke the work of John Bowlby and others on the need for parents, or mothers, to be at home with young children. These kinds of publications generate fierce debates in the Dutch media. Advoc- ates and opponents – in both cases often women – discuss emotionally the pros and cons of day care centres. The position of the growing number of employed mothers in The Netherlands therefore remains vulnerable. The recent economic recession has also resulted in declining government and employer funding and support for childcare services. Thus, it may become more expensive for individual parents, which could make paid work less attractive in financial terms for middle- and lower-earning women.

The prevalence of part-time work among women is also one reason why they continue to be seriously underrepresented in senior and visible jobs. The Government has initiated a series of female emancipation programmes in place since 1974, but our participants felt that there is little sense of urgency about the need to change. Rather than women wanting to work full-time, our participants suggest that many women would also like men to work less. If this trend develops it may not only challenge assumptions about men and women's roles, but also values concerning paid work and achievement.

NORWAY

Looking Backwards: Potential Levers for Change

Compared with other Scandinavian countries, Norway has historically tended to offer more public supports for women as mothers rather than as paid workers.[51] However, this stance has changed somewhat in recent decades and Norway now has one of the highest rates of female labour market participation in the world, with more and more women occupied in full-time employment.[52] Over time, a substantial increase in the level of education attained

---

[50] Thanks to Laura Den Dulk for a verbal translation of this.

[51] Sainsbury (2001) explores the ways in which women's positions in Norway and Sweden have diverged and developed over time. Reasons include the extent of women's organising capacities and the ways benefits were given on the basis of mother or worker roles in the different countries. She notes that in Norway, fewer policies have been directed to married women and mothers to support their labour market participation compared with other Scandinavian countries. So a slower growth of women in paid employment and their weaker attachment to it can be seen historically. However, while variations still exist, there has been convergence across Scandinavia since the 1990s. See Fagnani (2004) for a recent comparison looking at the specific context of work–family reconciliation.

[52] Sixty-nine per cent of all women compared with 77 per cent of all men are active in paid work. Although more women are also occupied in full-time work, many still work part-time hours (albeit longer part-time hours than in countries such as the UK and The Netherlands). See http://odin.dep.no/odin/engelsk/norway/social/032091-991525/index-dok000-b-n-a.html for a useful summary of women's position in Norway.

by women, together with smaller families, government-subsidised childcare places and increasing lengths of parental leave, for both men and women, have made it possible for many women to participate fully in paid working life and increasingly for men to participate more in family life.

Norway has long had a strong commitment to equality between men and women, as elsewhere in Scandinavia. The reasons for this commitment to equality are very complex but a novel argument was provided by one of our Norwegian participants, a specialist in equity issues between men and women. She suggests that the commitment to gender equity may be related to the outdoor culture of Norway.

> 'Women were always equal with men in terms of the hard work and the heavy physical loads they carried. The "little woman" image has never held much sway' (Norwegian woman, academic).

The main levers for change are government concerns about gender equity, alongside more general commitments to social equality, and about children's needs and well-being. 'Business' concerns, which are more important drivers of change towards more optimal harmonisations of paid work with other parts of life in other countries, have been more in the background.

Government Responses

The state has taken a lead in promoting equality between men and women, and in redistributing wealth with the effect of reducing income gaps between rich and poor. There is a consensus that the Government should take a lead in promoting gender equity through social regulation: an approach that has been termed 'state feminism' (see Leira, 1992). More recently, state policies have also actively encouraged men's greater involvement in family life. Men, especially fathers are encouraged to take an equitable share of the benefits and burdens of paid work and family life. A one-month period of parental leave introduced in 1993, commonly known as the 'daddy month', is assigned to men in two parent families on a 'use it or lose it' basis. If men do not take it, the family loses this month of parental leave. Most men now consider it a matter of course to use at least part of this allotted leave, and take-up of at least part of this leave in 2003 was 80 per cent.

Recent policy initiatives have attempted to ease some of the pressures connected with harmonising work with other parts of life, at least for parents of young children, by extending flexibility and choice for parents via a 'time-account' scheme. This gives parents the opportunity to work shorter hours without a reduction in income until the child is 2 or 3 years old. However, this has been less successful than the 'daddy month' in changing men's behaviour because it depends on negotiations between fathers and their managers (see Brandth & Kvande, 2002). This relates to a generic finding in all our countries: when flexibility has to be negotiated at an individual level it is much less likely to be effective than universal entitlements or wider changes in culture and practice. A 'cash for home care' policy, as an alternative to day care, has also been introduced. However, this is controversial as it is perceived as encouraging mothers to stay at home.

Workplaces

In the context of strong legislation and regulations for employee protection, there has been less need for workplace policies, although the need to accommodate parental leaves has encouraged employers to develop flexible working practices. While pockets of awareness about the potential benefits of flexible working are emerging, there are currently many gaps between policy and practice as there are in all the countries. It seems that at present there is limited awareness of the need to accompany workplace changes with wider shifts in workplace cultures and practices. For example, many private sector organisations competing in the global economy continue to define commitment in terms of time spent in the workplace (Brandth & Kvande, 2002). As a result, while more and more fathers say they want to work less so as to be more involved with the care of their children, it remains unusual for them to ask if they can work shorter hours.

Despite the rise of women in paid work, Norway has a very segregated labour market in terms of the types of work men and women tend to be involved in. This contributes to pay gaps between men and women as the kinds of work in which men tend to dominate are higher paid. It also holds back much potential change in working cultures and practices in male dominated professions. Given awareness about the importance of involving men in family life, recent Government initiatives to facilitate more women in senior jobs and sectors such as science have emerged as well as initiatives to increase the representation of women on boards of directors.

Looking Forwards: Potential Levers for Change?

The context for harmonising paid work with other parts of life seems relatively ideal. Yet both male and female participants talk about pressures they feel to 'have and do it all' in paid work and family life. Despite the commitments to gender equality and provisions and regulations to make the labour market more 'family-friendly', our participants say they experience stress and increasing life intensity and some see links between these pressures and rising divorce rates as well as sickness leaves, which are becoming new levers for change.

Other demographic issues, such as ageing populations, have also surfaced recently. As people live longer, pension entitlements are more expensive. There is also concern about the pressures and intensity of paid employment, which have resulted in early retirement packages. These have to be subsidised by workplace organisations, so our participants feel that this will become a major problem for employers in the coming years. Against this backdrop, some of our participants think that regulations and policies are not enough and employers will have to turn their attention to working practices that account for and respect diversity of people's needs and abilities, particularly as they change throughout the life course.

As workplaces become more exposed to global economic competition, even taking up the full one-month leave by fathers can be frowned on. As elsewhere, flexibility is often used to encourage people to work more rather than less. This perpetuates problems for women in terms of progress in paid work as well as problems for men in relation to time available for their families.

Norway, through its 'state feminist' approach, has made considerable strides in supporting equitable harmonisations of paid work with other parts of life, motivated by a commitment to social and gender equity and a high level of consensus for this. Our participants are proud of this. Yet, in light of global pressures to be ever more 'efficient', despite their strong history of a collective consensus for equality, participants say they feel increasingly powerless to make further changes to optimise ways in which they harmonise paid work with other parts of life. Many also feel concerned about protecting the progress that has been made so far in relation to gender equity and harmonising paid work with other parts of life in the context of trends such as the intensification of work, the focus on profits and rising consumerism. All this makes it more difficult to deal with further evolutions of equity between men and women and the difficult identity issues this involves. There is also concern that these trends and pressures challenge the very foundations and values on which Norwegian society has long been based.

Our country snapshots highlight that potential levers for change that have emerged since the 1950s, government and workplace responses, as well as current and emerging challenges and potential levers for change, are diverse. Contexts differ, but many of the underlying pressures and tensions are similar. Paid work is becoming more demanding for many people and there is concern about the impact this has on other parts of life. Assumptions about men and women's roles and relationships are centrally bound up with this. We explore the ways in which the underlying pressures and tensions manifest themselves in different contexts in more depth in Part II. But first, in the next chapter, we discuss the need for change at multiple levels and set out the concepts we use to explore these challenges: equity, well-being and sustainability.

CHAPTER 3

Thinking about Change at Multiple Levels

In this chapter we discuss the assumptions, concepts and approaches that influence the questions we ask and the interpretations of our findings. We begin by examining the language used to discuss the ways people combine paid work and other parts of life and the reasons why we believe current terminology needs to change. We then pick up on our argument from the last chapter that certain social and economic forces are potential levers for change in each country. These forces could drive change in different directions and so we consider criteria for optimal outcomes of change in the connections between paid work and other parts of life. Finally, we look at processes of change.

THE LIMITATIONS OF A 'WORK–LIFE BALANCE' APPROACH

'Work–life balance' has emerged as a widely used and popular way of talking about challenges of combining paid work with other parts of life.[1] This terminology originated in the USA and the UK and is now spreading to numerous other western as well as non-western countries, such as India and Japan. The terminology is often picked up via multinational corporations that have 'work–life' programmes and employee surveys that include items on 'work–life balance'. In this way, the dominance of the west, particularly of the USA, is reflected not only in the exportation of working practices that tend to preclude time and energy for activities beyond paid work, but also in the language used to discuss these problems.

A shift in terminology from 'work–family' and 'family-friendly policies' to 'work–life' and 'work–life balance' occurred as growing numbers of men and women experienced more demanding working practices and environments leading to feelings of pressure, lack of time and general 'busyness'. This shift in language reflects a broader and more inclusive way of framing the debate that attempts to engage men and women with and without young children or other caring commitments.

We contend, however, that while 'work–life balance' terminology is potentially more inclusive, it paints a superficial and oversimplistic picture of the many challenges it seeks to address. It appears to suggest that work is not a part of life. Yet paid work – although often too much of a part – is a necessary and often meaningful and rewarding aspect of life for many people. The language of 'work–life balance' also ignores distinctions

---

[1] In Europe, the language of reconciling employment with family life is also common but some Europeans increasingly use 'work–life balance' too.

between paid and unpaid work, and further undervalues unpaid care work by implying that it is just another part of the 'non-work' domain. The idea that it is possible to get the right balance between work and other parts of life also overlooks the shifting nature of people's work and non-work involvements and the meanings given to these activities across the life course (Moen & Sweet, 2004). The word 'balance' implies a trade-off – one side goes up, the other goes down – yet work and personal life are not necessarily antithetical or mutually exclusive. Indeed there is growing evidence suggesting that a workplace focus on employees' needs and wishes beyond the workplace may also enhance workplace effectiveness.[2] Yet the word 'balance' glosses over the many ways in which paid work and personal lives may feed into, affect, or enhance each other in diverse ways across the life course.

The language used to talk about combining paid work with other parts of life is crucial: oversimplification limits possible responses. The very language that has helped to raise awareness about some paid work and personal life issues now seems to be a barrier to thinking more widely about how things might change.

HARMONISING PAID WORK WITH OTHER PARTS OF LIFE

We realise that the terminology used will continue to evolve but at present, we suggest that thinking about multiple challenges in terms of harmonising paid work with other parts of life might encourage wider and more radical thinking. This approach implies that activities associated with paid work, unpaid care and domestic work, friendship, leisure activities and community participation are interrelated and not necessarily antithetical to each other, or needing to be 'balanced'.

When we began our research we used the language of integrating paid work with other parts of life but we encountered some resistance to the term integration. In the context of the growing blurring of boundaries between paid work and other activities, some people prefer to experience paid work and other parts of life in more separated or segregated ways and feel that integration suggests too much overlap. So we began, instead, to talk about harmonising paid work with other parts of life. There are a variety of different ways to harmonise the many parts of life, including more integrated or segregated strategies, depending on what works for people in diverse contexts and at different phases in their lives.[3] What is important is that men and women have maximum options unconstrained by notions that, for example, paid work *should* be separate from other parts of life, or that men *should* be more attached to paid work and women to family responsibilities.

In our introduction, we argued that harmonising paid work with other parts of life is of central importance for individuals, families, organisations, communities and societies as a whole in the current global economy. This points to the need for a broader approach to harmonising paid work with other parts of life; one that considers optimal outcomes at many different levels. We conceptualise optimal change in terms of equity, impact on well-being and sustainability.

---

[2] See, for example some of our own work documenting innovative approaches for change, Rapoport et al. (2002) and Lewis and Cooper (2005). These approaches focus on more systemic strategies, which engage in mutual processes of collaboration between employees and employers in devising working strategies that may enhance – or have no negative effects – on workplace performance and productivity.

[3] See also Esping-Andersen (2002). He uses the language of harmonising in the context of work–personal life issues and challenges for welfare states.

EQUITY: A SOCIAL JUSTICE APPROACH

First, we assume that optimal changes at the individual level and in families, workplaces, communities and wider societies will be those that enable people to harmonise paid work with other parts of life in equitable ways – in ways that are experienced as *fair*.

Social justice theories distinguish between the principles of equality, need and equity.[4] Equality implies that people should be treated the same regardless of needs; need implies that people in certain situations, such as mothers and fathers with young children, should be given special supports; and equity, while incorporating need, is focused more broadly on perceived fairness. We use equity rather than equality in relation to harmonising paid work with other parts of life because people have multiple and varied needs and responsibilities at various points in their life course. Men and women in relationships need to deal with their needs in ways that they feel are equitable at different stages in their life course. For them to be able to do this without undue constraints, depends on social and organisational structures, cultures and practices that support the widest range of options. For example, partners may feel it is equitable to share childcare and economic provision equally, or to take it in turns to prioritise one or the other. For this to be possible there has to be: (1) social policy support for fathers and mothers to share parental leaves; (2) workplace values and practices that do not penalise employees who work less than full-time, or take leaves from work, at particular points in the life course; and (3) wider societal norms that value both paid work and caring as legitimate activities for both men and women.

In this book we focus primarily on equity between men and women, as this form of equity is central for understanding challenges in harmonising paid work with other parts of life. However, equity between men and women is notoriously difficult to define.

At the individual level people define for themselves what they experience as fair, although this is influenced by what they feel entitled to expect at home and at work, which, in turn, is influenced by societal contexts and what is perceived as 'normal' and feasible (see, for example, Lewis & Smithson, 2001). Wider societal debates about equity between men and women are often couched in terms of a particular dilemma: should equity be approached via measures that enable women to become like men, or should it be approached by provisions that respond to the specific circumstances of women as mothers or carers?[5] In other words, should strategies emphasise women's similarity to men or their difference? Yet Nancy Fraser argues, in the context of welfare policies and wider societal shifts, that neither approach will ever be sufficient for true equity between men and women as neither fully challenges workplace assumptions about 'ideal' workers or requires or enables men to change.[6] Instead, she reflects on a third possible approach that includes measures at multiple levels of society to enable *both* men and women to have more oppor-

---

[4] For a more detailed account of this, see Lewis and Haas (2005), who provide a discussion of social justice theories and approaches in the context of combining paid work with other parts of life.

[5] For discussions of these dilemmas in the context of welfare provisions, see Pateman (1988) and Fraser (1997). For more generic discussions of these dilemmas, see Scott (1996).

[6] Fraser (1997) explores the limitations of these approaches for gender equity by exploring two ideal type scenarios for welfare provisions and supports: the Universal Breadwinner model and the Caregiver Parity model. On the basis of seven different principles for gender equity (anti-poverty, anti-exploitation, income equality, leisure time equality, equality of respect, anti-marginalisation and anti-androcentrism) she finds neither model is fully sufficient as neither asks men or workplaces to change significantly.

tunities to combine paid work with other parts of life, including family, community and leisure activities. This approach encourages a potentially fairer allocation of opportunities and constraints for men and women and thus perceived equity between them.[7]

Although our major focus is on equity between men and women, the impact of other forms of diversity, such as social class, income, sexuality, ethnicity, culture, disability, age and phase in the life course on experiences of harmonising paid work with other parts of life are also very important. These interact in a number of ways with equity between men and women. For example, women are more likely to experience poverty than men, and this reflects assumptions that women should be more involved with family care, often together with limited public support for these responsibilities.[8]

WELL-BEING

We assume that the ultimate goal of social and economic development is positive well-being and quality of life. Optimal changes to support the harmonisation of paid work with other parts of life should contribute to individual and social well-being in equitable and sustainable ways.

Current research increasingly focuses on positive well-being, that is, something that is more than simply the absence of stress or illness, but rather involves positive enjoyment and pleasure (see, for example, Bryce & Haworth, 2002; Delle Fave & Massimini, 2003). We focus here on physical and psychological aspects of positive well-being as well as economic and material well-being. These do not necessarily go hand in hand as people living in the richest societies are not necessarily the happiest (see Layard, 2003; 2005). We will return to this point later in Chapter 6.

Participation in paid work can be a vital source of well-being at many different levels (see, for example, Barnett, 1998; Frone, Yardley & Markel, 1997; Lewis, Kagan & Heaton, 2000; Marks, 1977). Apart from income, it can also contribute to a sense of identity, fulfill social needs and often contribute to personal growth, as we discuss in Chapter 4. However, much depends on the nature of work. At one extreme paid work can be crucial for survival but can involve conditions over which people have no control that can make it difficult to harmonise with other basic needs such as caring for family members (Heymann et al., 2004). At the other extreme, some of the people we spoke with in our study said they enjoyed working very long hours and argue that this is one way of harmonising paid work and other parts of life that contributes to their well-being. Nevertheless, excessive workloads, while satisfying for some, at least in the short-term can deplete energy as well as time for other activities, reduce well-being and increase stress-related illnesses, especially if these workloads are externally imposed, but often also if they are apparently 'freely chosen' (Sparks et al., 1997). Work-related stress is increasingly discussed in the media in many countries – an example of social forces exerting mounting pressures for change.

---

[7] See, for example, Rapoport and Rapoport (1975), which offers an early discussion of conceptualisation challenges and actual experiences.

[8] For a succinct account of women's experiences of poverty compared with men see Daly (1992). For a more detailed and illustrated account, see Daly and Rake (2003). Both texts also discuss different reasons why women are likely to be poorer than men, including the vulnerability of female-headed households as well as the hidden poverty women can experience because of inequitable household resource allocations between men and women. For detailed discussions and differing perspectives of intra-household resource distribution between men and women see Pahl (1989) and Curtis (1986).

Moreover, the invasiveness of paid work in people's lives – whether because of intense demands and expectations, the addictiveness of some types of work, or because of economic necessity – may have implications not only for individual well-being but also for the well-being of families and communities, as we discuss in Chapter 5. Limited opportunities to participate in activities outside paid work may also, ultimately, impact negatively on workplaces. For example, relationships and interpersonal skills, which are increasingly required in many forms of paid work,[9] are often developed through domestic or care responsibilities or interactions with other family members or friends in personal as well as workplace settings. Workplaces as well as families and communities require people to have a sense of well-being if they are to be effective and sustainable.

SUSTAINABILITY

Optimal changes in the ways that people can harmonise paid work with other parts of life will also be those that are sustainable. Sustainability is often considered in the context of the physical environment and the economy, but increasingly also in terms of the social environment more generally, including, for example, the growing interest in sustainable communities. Our discussions of sustainability refer to the social environment and economy as well as human sustainability.

How sustainable are working practices that overlook the diversity of the workforce and continue to assume that ideal workers can work as if they have no other responsibilities? How sustainable are societies in which the birth rate has fallen well below replacement levels – a trend that has been associated with the difficulty men and women experience in harmonising paid work with family responsibilities in equitable ways.[10] How sustainable are communities in the context of declining participation in local activities, which some commentators have linked to changes in the value and practice of paid work?[11] How sustainable is democratic legitimacy if lack of time and energy attributed to current working practices threatens civic spirit and political participation (see, for example, Blunkett, 2001; Voydanoff, 2004)?

Against this backdrop, there is a need for debate that goes far beyond short-term considerations of 'work–life balance' towards one that addresses long-term issues of sustainability as well as equity and quality of life. As Juliet Webster (2004, pp. 62–63) argues, 'we now have to broaden our concerns to consider the impact of the organisation of work on the wider sphere of life beyond paid employment – for the individual, for communities, for society at large. In other words, our concern must now be with enhancing the broader social sustainability of working life'.

---

[9] See Fletcher (1999). Another example is given by Sennett (1998), who discusses the ways in which current ways of working require particular value sets that seem inconsistent with the values required in family and personal life and thus contribute to a 'corrosion of character'.

[10] For example, Castles (2003) explores the reasons for fertility decline and some examples of reversals of these trends in countries including Scandinavian countries and suggests supportive family-friendly policies can help contribute towards reversing fertility decline trends. Cooke (forthcoming, 2006) also explores the extent to which equitable relationships and role distributions exist between men and women and finds that more equitable divisions of labour can increase the chance of couples experiencing a second birth.

[11] See Putnam (2000), for example, in which he offers an exhaustive account of the decline of community participation in the USA.

MAKING CHANGES

Bringing about optimal change in the ways that people can harmonise paid work and other parts of life in equitable, satisfying and sustainable ways will require not only social and workplace policies addressing 'work–life balance', but also deeper changes at individual, family, community, workplaces and wider societal levels. We conceptualise the kinds of changes that may be required in terms of *processes* to achieve *systemic* change at *multiple* and *connected* levels. Change in any one sphere has a knock-on effect on other spheres. Changes in the workplace, for example, impact on experiences of families and communities and vice versa. When thinking about change at any one level therefore – in men–women relationships, families, workplaces, communities or wider societies – it is important to also consider the impacts on other levels, and the ways in which other levels or systems will need to change. For example government policies to encourage changes in families, to enable fathers to be more involved with children, require changes in workplace practices and values. The success of such policies might also require changes in values and practices at the community level, for example in assumptions made about parenting by staff in schools and health centres, and in the timing of civic activities.

Policies aiming to support people in combining paid work with other parts of their lives often have limited impact, not only because they fail to address the need for change at multiple levels, but also because the changes that they aim for in any one sphere, are too superficial. They do not address *systemic* change. By systemic change we mean changes in practices, structures and cultures (including values and norms) that reward certain behaviour and characteristics over others. Social systems (for example, workplaces, families, communities) embody rules, cultures and assumptions about how work – paid or unpaid – can be most effectively carried out. This affects the way things are done in practice, for example workplace practices, or the way domestic and caring work is apportioned and carried out. Often assumptions that may have been functional at one time persist inappropriately. For example, assumptions about the best way of getting work done that may have been appropriate in the context of less diverse labour forces, with less advanced technology, are unlikely to be appropriate now, but often persist unquestioned and continue to influence expectations. The goal of systemic change is to bring about change in the rules and assumptions within any system so that more appropriate ways of getting things done can be developed. For example, in workplaces, assumptions that 'ideal' workers do not need time for family involvement are based on the out-dated belief that most workers have full-time 'wives' or equivalent at home to take care of family matters and do not need or wish to modify work for family reasons. Bringing about systemic change is not easy. It cannot be achieved simply by changing the rules without changing people's assumptions and values, for example introducing flexi-time systems in workplaces without changing the belief that ideal workers do not need flexibility. Systemic change involves getting beyond quick fixes and focusing on change processes. These will differ according to context. There is no one size fits all process, although there are certain generic principles. These include: the need for people to engage in deep, collaborative thinking about what may be possible or desirable; reflection on persisting assumptions and their impact; action to bring about desired change; and continual collaborative reflection to move beyond resistances or unforeseen difficulties as change occurs.

Collaborative and interactive action-orientated research within leading edge companies in the USA carried out by Rhona Rapoport, Lotte Bailyn and colleagues (Rapoport et al., 2002) to promote a dual agenda of enhancing workplace effectiveness and promoting equitable and sustainable ways of combining paid work and personal life provides an example of a process approach to systemic change, at the workplace level. This has had some success. The process involved working collaboratively with employees to examine working practices and the values and assumptions on which they are based, examining the impact on employees and on workplace effectiveness, and thinking collaboratively about alternative ways of working. Significantly, both employee needs and wishes *and* workplace effectiveness must be considered together for this process to be effective. If a focus on either workplace effectiveness or equity is dropped, outcomes are less successful.

The limits of individual change without change at the systemic level are recognised in this approach – change must take place at the systemic and collective level. Nevertheless, change amongst certain influential individuals can be critical for systemic change in workplace cultures and practices to take place. For example, Rapoport, Bailyn and colleagues discussed the reluctance of one manager to enable dual agenda changes amongst his work group which held back progress. Over time, in the context of discussing his anxieties, which were fed back to him in constructive ways, he became more open to change. Something in the process of working through deeply held – but outdated – assumptions had changed his mindset. He went on to empower his work group to make changes that could enhance workplace effectiveness as well as enabling them to have more time or energy for other parts of their lives. Thus, change at the individual level, alongside change at the systemic level, is critical and part and parcel of a process-orientated approach to dual agenda change. Yet this can feel threatening, painful and difficult.

As Rapoport, Bailyn and colleagues (2002, p. 168) point out:

> change at the level of work practices is difficult because it challenges the importance of work in people's lives. It requires dealing with 'mind sets' and feelings about commitment and competence that support established ways of working, as well as the prominence of paid work in life. Such entrenched beliefs are particularly hard to deal with – even talk about in work groups – because they touch on men's and women's sense of identity and self esteem.

Thus experiences in the workplace interact with deep identity issues perpetuated in men–women relationships, in families and other relationships as well as in communities and wider societies.

This is one approach to process-orientated dual agenda change at the workplace level. There will be other approaches to dual agenda systemic change in workplaces and these processes can be applied at other levels. Systemic process-orientated approaches are also important at family and community levels, in which assumptions about 'ideal' mothers, fathers or carers often hold back change.[12] Change processes are important but other supports remain important for optimum harmonisation of paid work and other parts of life, including support from government policies. At the same time, systemic process-orientated approaches are also important in government policy making. Optimum change will involve systemic changes at multiple and related levels.

Changes will happen, nothing remains static. But if the various potential levers for change that we discussed in Chapter 2 are to contribute to more equitable, satisfying and sustainable ways of harmonising paid work with other parts of life, 'norms' and assumptions that operate at different levels of society will need to be unpacked and explored.

---

[12] See also Degroot and Fine (2003), who discuss ways in which they have engaged and worked collaboratively with men and women to overcome identity, cultural and structural barriers to shared care approaches.

Attention to process approaches for more fundamental dual agenda systemic change is not easy and does not foster quick fix solutions. A process approach recognises and works with notions that issues of harmonising the many parts of life are highly complex and involve multiple actors at multiple levels engaging in deep, collaborative thinking, reflection and action. Such an approach may sound difficult and time consuming but if equity, well-being and sustainability of people and societies are to be valued, it may be increasingly necessary.

So this is our position. In the chapters that follow, we explore the many connections between the different parts of life and draw on our research to document contemporary challenges of harmonising paid work with family and personal life.

PART II

Making the Connections

In this part of the book we delve deeper into our data to illustrate and probe contemporary experiences, tensions and dilemmas connected with harmonising paid work with other parts of life. We explore this against a backdrop of what we call the five Cs:

- current forms of capitalism
- consumerism
- commitment
- care
- connectedness.

Current dominant and influential forms of neo-liberal capitalism, which place an emphasis on the primacy of the unfettered free market, encourage demanding workplace expectations and prevailing notions of commitment that are exacerbated by the lure of accumulation and consumerism. In this context, people can experience paid work in ways that undermine time and energy for care giving and receiving, which can threaten people's well-being and connectedness with others across all areas of life. Current contexts and experiences of paid work may also be detrimental for long-term workplace effectiveness and sustainability.

In Chapter 4 we explore contemporary experiences of paid work and changes that are contributing to contemporary 'work–life' pressures. In Chapter 5 we explore the ways in which paid work experiences relate to experiences of care at family, friendship and community levels, as well as care of the self – including time for leisure and rest. In Chapter 6 we look at relationships between men and women and how this relates to challenges about harmonising the many parts of life in equitable, satisfying and sustainable ways.

CHAPTER 4

The Invasiveness of Paid Work

There is concern in all the seven countries covered in this book about the growing dominance of paid work in people's lives.

> . . . in our industry you cannot not take a call, my cell phone has to be on because in a process escalation if there is a real problem . . . at that time my cell phone can't be off . . . the companies we work with they have all the reasons why they don't want to work out of India and you don't want to give them one more reason. (Indian woman, call centre manager)

> Something is fundamentally wrong, perhaps our workaholism, which has misaligned us in ways that act against our own principles. People feel helpless to do anything about what has happened to themselves and their families. (US woman in our country meeting)

> If you work in a company you have to spend your life more or less at work. You work and work and work. (Norwegian man, formerly working for a large company, now freelance)

> The workload is the primary source of stress, which impacts on the work-home interface . . . we need to integrate community, family, spirituality and leisure. We have lost perspective. Yes we live to work, not work to live. Work is the goal of life at the moment, but this is wrong. (South African man in our country meeting)

In this chapter we focus on people's experiences of paid work, assumptions about 'ideal' workers and ways in which these assumptions are exacerbated by changes in the nature of work and workplaces operating in a global context. We focus on experiences of paid work largely connected to workplace organisations. However, this includes not only the experiences of employers and employees but also, increasingly, other people who are more informally attached, such as freelancers, consultants, outsourced or peripheral workers. At the same time, experiences of paid work in formal organisations more generally also affect many people throughout society regardless of their direct employment relationship. Although not the focus of this chapter, people such as Enrika, for example, who is Elizabeth's nanny in the US-based opening story, are affected by organisational structures, cultures and practices: Enrika is affected by the expectations and values inherent within Elizabeth's workplace and has to be available for her employers' children for long hours despite serious implications for her own personal life.

ASSUMPTIONS ABOUT 'IDEAL' WORKERS

In many contexts, especially among professionals and managers, ideal workers are regarded as those who demonstrate 'commitment' in terms of long hours and exclusive dedication to the job. In other forms of work, where unpaid overtime is not expected, ideal workers nevertheless tend to be regarded as those who work full-time, intensively, and do not modify work for family or other reasons. Yet workforces are increasingly diverse and 'ideal' worker assumptions are problematic for growing numbers of people. While lip-service is frequently paid to the differing needs of people with caring commitments, it is often assumed that only women need time for family or other care activities. Less attention is given to needs and responsibilities men may have in terms of family commitments and so 'ideal' workers assumptions can create problems for men as well as women. In addition, there is more diversity in terms of age, disability and other factors, which could also challenge assumptions about 'ideal' workers. For example, as populations age, people may want to work longer but less intensively over the life course. Even within the age group of 'young people', some want to work a great deal while others would rather experience life with less work for a while. Although these needs tend to receive limited attention, there are some indications of pockets of change. For example, in a context where a high percentage of the adult working age population is affected by HIV/AIDS, a South African man explains that: 'When a person has reached a point of being unable to fulfil their normal work functions, then they need to be accommodated with a shorter working day. Those kinds of adjustments are being built into policies in workplaces.' However, he goes on to question how much impact these adjustments can have in the context of pervasive 'ideal' worker expectations.

Assumptions about commitment in terms of willingness and ability to work full-time or to put in long hours at the workplace are relatively recent. Prior to the industrial revolution, a good working day was often equated with task and seasonal time. As we discussed in Chapter 2, with the rise of industrialisation, work and family came to be regarded as separate spheres, with paid work associated more with men and family more with women. Workplaces were thus developed primarily around the needs of men. 'Ideal' workers came to be defined as those who could prioritise paid work and often as those who displayed stereotypically 'male' attributes such as aggressive go-getting characteristics (see, for example, Bailyn & Harrington, 2004; Lewis, 1997; Rapoport et al., 2002). Forms of paid work such as part-time work or certain occupations that tend to be female dominated, which allow workers to make time for other things, tend to be undervalued. Thus assumptions about 'ideal' workers make it difficult for 'non-ideal' workers – those who have other commitments – to participate and advance in certain occupations, or for those who are particularly career-focused to become more involved in unpaid family or community activities.

IDEAL WORKERS AND THE CURRENT GLOBAL ECONOMY

While hours in paid work declined in many countries over the past century as a result of emerging social rights and trade union demands, such as 'eight hours for work, eight hours for sleep, and eight hours for play', these trends have been reversed in post-industrial contexts (Perrons, 2003). Far from the once predicted rise of a leisured society, many people across a range of different countries are again working long and intensive hours. Many people across the world work long hours, simply to make ends meet and this is not restricted to 'developing' countries:

> 'Many Americans are working long hours, often in multiple jobs, just to keep going financially' (American man, politician).

In this chapter, however, we focus on those people in the seven countries who have to work long and hard to get through heavy workloads – a common phenomenon in a range of occupations[1] – as well as those who have to be seen to put in long hours of what, in the USA is called 'face time', to demonstrate 'commitment'.

> There is a tendency for people to think long hours make you look like [you are] adding value. But it is just a perception, which is false, and perpetuates a way of work. You work long hours, and then you are seen as really making a difference. (attendee at South Africa country meeting)
>
> . . . it has become so entrenched . . . especially in the new economy . . . we've got to work hard and give up all our, you know, literally give up our personal lives. (India, management consultant)

Many of our participants volunteered that the widespread tendency to regard 'ideal' workers as those who can not only work long and hard but also display stereotypically masculine characteristics appears to be growing.

> I'm afraid it's got worse. I don't think it was so bad 20 years ago, but now, the long hours, the aggressive looking after your career, moving around for your career. I think it's got a lot worse . . . I don't think a gentle laid back even bright intelligent person will get ahead in the kind of society we have now . . . if they don't have as a part and parcel of their armoury a kind of assertive aggressive nature, they're not going to make it. I think it's sad, I think it's really sad. (British manager)

So why is it that so many people feel they have to work long and intensive hours? To answer this question we must consider some of the many changes that have taken place in the nature and organisation of work. Many of these developments are double-edged. They have the potential to support more optimal harmonising of paid work with other parts of life by providing more flexibility. Yet recent developments can also enable and encourage people to work harder. These changes include: developments in technology; efficiency drives; and new management practices. All these relate to the global 24/7 economy and the spread of current forms of neo-liberal competitive capitalism, but they are also reflected in public sector workplaces.

Technology

The rise of information and communication technology has revolutionised the ways that many people work. On the positive side, work can be processed and delivered more quickly. Growing numbers of people can participate in well-paid and/or interesting jobs from locations such as their own homes using the internet, computer networking and other equipment. Technology also offers means of communication to those who would otherwise be isolated. This challenges the separation between work and home and has the potential to radically alter the ways in which paid work is carried out. Yet technology has done little to reduce the amounts of time and energy many people spend in paid work. Instead,

---

[1] See Transitions Research Report #3 (2004), which documents findings that feelings of intensification of work as a common experience in a series of 11 organisational case studies in the public and private sectors across seven European countries. See www.workliferesearch.org/transitions for more publications and discussions.

with trends that call for ever more 'efficient' ways of working, technology often results in people working longer and at a faster pace. Responses to emails, faxes and other communications are often required immediately, speeding up work process and contributing to the feelings of busyness and time urgency.

As people work across time zones they often feel that they have to be constantly available. Working remotely, especially from home, can enhance flexibility to fit in other activities but can also enable people to work all the time. For example, Anna in our Dutch story spends evenings at home replying to emails from colleagues in the USA. Many people talk about the tyranny of email, which appears to increase the extent of communications.

> 'New ways of working are being vaulted onto the old ways of working, rather than replacing them. People email from home, work across time zones, use laptops, but most people still go to work at 8 o'clock every morning and work a 12-hour day' (British man, researcher).

Technology has also increasingly replaced certain roles, such as secretaries, so many people who would have delegated certain tasks, now incorporate these into their everyday schedules. Moreover, people are so reliant on technology that when it goes wrong they experience extreme stress and frustration. Technology enables people to work across time zones, with positive as well as negative consequences in 'developing' as well as 'developed' countries.

> India is going to be the hub for business process outsourcing for ITES, software etc . . . and that will put even more pressure on us, in terms of time differences in the time zones and in terms of more unsecured professions today. (Indian businessman at country meeting)

> We are feeding mostly into the US . . . so the US wakes up when we are about to sleep so it's normally the evening and night work . . . employees that come into the job are young people immediately out of college or university and just about to start their career and then they are working and starting at 4 or 5 o'clock in the afternoon until 2 or 3 o'clock in the morning, so the working hours itself is a work and personal life imbalance issue because even if you go back home early morning you will sleep through the day and that happens a lot. (Indian man, employee)

Hence, despite the changes and potential that technology brings for greater harmonisation of paid work with personal life, the dominance of paid work in many people's lives has actually increased.

Downsizing, Efficiency and Maximizing Profits

In the context of global competition, many private and public sector organisations downsize to become more 'efficient', which increases individual workloads and the pace of work. This is a widespread phenomenon found in all seven countries, as well as others. In another ongoing study looking at changing European workplaces (including two former Eastern bloc case studies: Bulgaria and Slovenia), employees at various levels in public and private sector organisations report an intensification of work (see www.work-liferesearch.org/transitions). Intensification of work affects manual workers as well as white collar workers, as we saw in the example of Zhilah's husband, a miner in our South African opening story.[2]

Downsizing and 'efficiency' trends are also associated with an increase in perceived or actual job insecurity. This increases feelings of pressure, which can lead to a tendency to overwork while employment is available and can sometimes lead to stress and burn-out.

> Some men have problems . . . because of the huge pressures of both getting a good job and the pressures that come with the job, such as long hours and growing insecurity about the future. (Japanese woman, researcher)

> [If] people can't predict if they will be in this job tomorrow and what they will be earning next week, people will inevitably adapt a make hay while the sun shines attitude. 'I'd better work my butt off now because I don't know if I'll have these opportunities tomorrow.' (US politician)

> Fears of unemployment; contract workers being exploited; poverty and inequality issues . . . all lead to stress and burn-out. (South African, country meeting)

The outsourcing of low level work by organisations – absolving workplace responsibility for these workers who are excluded from workplace 'family-friendly' or 'work–life' policies – is associated with a growth of employment agencies in many countries. Often people with caring or other commitments say they 'choose' to do agency work because it gives them flexibility, but this is often at the expense of employment benefits and job security (Lambert, 1999).

Options to outsource work to other countries can also fuel to employee concerns, as we saw with David in our UK opening story. Thus, one of the effects of globalisation is that people in 'developed' countries may fear losing their jobs to the growing pool of global talent in 'developing' countries. Although employment is created in 'developing' countries, the flip side is that these jobs are also insecure (or perceived to be insecure). Hence, problems associated with western employment trends are also exported, despite the impacts on wider societies:

> 'Job insecurity is something that has come to stay . . . it is very traumatic socially, but we as a nation will have to learn to live with that' (Indian manager).

As discussed in Chapter 2, there is a view in India that there is no alternative to working long and intensive hours, whatever the social costs, if they are to develop economically to compete in the global economy:

> 'We have to be seen as being as smart and competitive as the West and we will have to keep on developing and thinking less of the social until we reach this' (Indian, manager).

Nevertheless, people in any of the seven countries are questioning the spread and inevitability of current forms of neo-liberal capitalism, which put profits before people. However, we did find some awareness about the problems of continuing in this way, which reflects a growing number of voices in academic and popular literature (see, for

---

[2] Gallie (2002) argues that 'there has been a sharp intensification of work effort, posing serious risks of work stress and tension between work and family life' (p. 97). Exploring the European context, and implications for welfare strategies, he finds increasing work pressure and expected work effort is experienced by people across different occupational or income classes. He argues that although evidence suggests work pressure and intensity may have increased most for those in higher skilled jobs, a wide body of research also finds that pressure can be particularly severe amongst the low skilled too. This is connected, in part, to a relative lack of control they may have over work task. When combined with high demands and expectations, this can have acute impacts on experiences of stress (pp. 105–106).

example, Bauman, 2003; Bunting, 2004; Clarke, 2004; Handy, 1997; Stiglitz, 2002; Webster, 2004).

> 'You have got that pressure which is really dumping on people in a way that perhaps wasn't the case 10 years ago or so . . . until we find some economic and social models, which enable people to proceed in some sort of parallel [with other things in life], we will be a bit stuck' (UK, corporate HR manager in a multinational company).

New Management Practices

The intensification of work is also exacerbated by contemporary management practices such as 'high commitment' or 'high performance' management approaches (Appelbaum & Berg, 2001; White, Hill, McGovern, Mills & Smeaton, 2003). These can be empowering but they often seek ways of encouraging and manipulating employees to put in extra 'discretionary' or voluntary effort and to internalise the need to work harder to improve performance. These approaches involve practices such as team working, target setting and financial incentives, for example performance-related pay. Such practices can be experienced very positively, contributing to job satisfaction and also potentially enhancing opportunities for harmonising paid work and other parts of life. However, many are also double-edged and can increase demands and intensity of work. The increasing use of team working, for example, particularly self-managing teams, can increase autonomy and flexibility but can also result in colleagues becoming agents of social control to ensure maximum effort. This is especially so when team working is combined with target setting.

> Employers . . . offer to pay miners a little more if they work longer and harder – bonuses are being linked to targets. People are paid overtime to achieve results, and it is the team members who collectively decide whether or not they should work longer or not. And this means that those wanting to work less are often silenced or stopped by peer pressure: more people, especially the young, want to work more. (South African, country meeting)

Self-managed teams can offer flexibility for people to deal with family crises or other personal needs, especially where feelings of reciprocity develop and colleagues cover for each other. Yet, in the contemporary context of intense workloads teamwork can often reduce flexibility: team members know that if they take time out of work for any reason their already overburdened colleagues will have to cover for them (Crompton, Dennett & Wigfield, 2003; Transitions Research Report #3, 2004).

New management practices are also associated with a growth in atypical working hours and flexible working arrangements, partly to meet employers' needs, for example to cover the 24/7 market place and sometimes to address the needs of workers in a range of occupations. However, atypical work is not necessarily flexible. Indeed, Diane Perrons (2003, p. 69) argues, 'flexible working seems to be more concerned with accommodating life to rather demanding and unquestioned working hours rather than one of reorganising work to allow time for domestic and caring responsibilities'. Flexible working arrangements can provide more autonomy about where and when work is carried out but this often depends on managers' motives and discretion.

> A lot of multinationals have come in and people have begun working in non-Indian organisations, I have been hearing more and more about work–life issues, the other day somebody was talking about flexi-hours and how she can convert an assignment into man hours and it doesn't matter if she does it from home . . . but I'm not sure how many Indian

> organisations would do that. I tried to do the same with the organisation I worked with and I wasn't successful . . . it wasn't okay with them. (Indian woman, manager)

Moreover, paradoxically, it is often the very workers who have most control over their own working hours and who can be flexible to fit in non-work activities that are under the most pressure and often use flexibility to work more rather than fewer hours (see Brandth & Kvande, 2001; Holt & Thaulow, 1996; Lewis, S., 2001; Lewis 2003a; Perlow, 1998).

Trades unions have responded to these trends in different ways in different countries. In Norway and The Netherlands, better conditions have often been negotiated via collective agreements. In Britain, although union membership is declining, the Trades Union Congress has taken initiatives to work collaboratively with some organisations to move towards greater flexibility of working arrangements (www.tuc.org.uk/changingtimes). In Japan, some unions are negotiating for shorter hours rather than higher pay. Unions overall, however, do not appear to have great power to hold back the insidious processes of the intensification of work. Across different contexts, many people feel obliged or compelled to give more energy, emotional labour, or 'more of themselves' to their paid work activities.[3]

INVASIVENESS OF PAID WORK

All of this contributes to an invasiveness of paid work. Yet many people talk about 'choosing' to work long and hard. Although some work still involves drudgery, conditions of work have improved for many people.

> For more people, work has got a lot better. It's impossible to claim it's getting worse. Average earnings have gone up . . . ; a third of us meet our friends through work; half of us meet our life partners through work. It can't be all that bad. The more post-industrial the workplace gets, the more people go into creative white collar jobs, then the more the line between what was once work and once leisure begins to blur. . . . A lot of the things we used to call leisure, such as talking to others, creating things, writing, reading, etc, well, that's the stuff of a lot of people's jobs now. Is it any wonder white collar workers are working such long hours? (British man, journalist)

In many ways contemporary work is becoming more satisfying and compelling. It can be inherently interesting and sociable and a major source of status and identity, as illustrated here with some UK observations.[4]

> We define ourselves by our working status . . . and for me; it gives me pleasure, status and meaning. (British woman, policy advisor)

> They used to tell me that on average people died 18 months after leaving the company. It was terrible. I mean you know without the organisation you were nothing, you lost your identity, your secretary and so on. You weren't anybody. (UK, Human Resources Director, male)

There are countless reasons why paid work can provide people with a sense of meaning and purpose. Many people with whom we spoke say they work hard because they believe they are 'making a difference', which can make such activities particularly compelling or addictive. People in our Indian country meeting spoke of Ghandi as an example of

---

[3] Webster (2004); see also Hochschild (1983), who first developed the concept of emotional labour, describing it as labour that 'requires one to induce or suppress feelings in order to sustain the outward countenance that produces the proper state of mind in others' (p. 7).

[4] On the positive side, paid work can be a tremendous source of self-esteem and well-being for individuals (Csikszentmihalyi, 1997).

someone who sacrificed his life to his work, often leaving his family for months or years on end. To use another example from South Africa, a black trades union representative told us that he worked all day and all night to bring an end to apartheid. Even post-apartheid he works long and intense hours as he feels there is so much that still needs to be done to transform society.

> I work long hours because I'm a servant. I work because I am a transformation agent, it's a call to help transform. That's what makes me tick. In areas where there is not much development, like Africa, it's a big problem. Now with the political stabilisation, there is a rush to develop Africa. And there is a lot of work to be done. (South African man, Trades Union)

Work can not only offer satisfaction, status and purpose, but also resources that may not be available elsewhere. At one extreme a Human Resources manager in India who carried out a survey to find out why so many people came in voluntarily on a Saturday told us:

> 'People come into work on Saturdays because there is no electricity at home, because they get a free lunch, the office is [an] air conditioned environment, they have access to the gym. People say they can sit and chat, use the Internet, and do a lot of things they can't do at home' (Indian woman, HR manager).

Another view is that people work hard to fulfil consumerist desires, even though this can be self-perpetuating.[5] As Madeleine Bunting (2004, p. 157) argues, 'the harder you work, the longer and the more intense your hours, the more pressure you experience, the more intense is the drive to repair, console, restore and find periodic escape through consumerism'. We hear widespread concerns about the impact of growing consumerism, for example among new economy workers in India as well as people in Norway, although there are pockets of awareness of the need to change here, too:

> We have become extremely greedy . . . I have a car, I want to go for a bigger car. I have a house, I want to go for a bigger house . . . I have two houses I want a third one because of my insecurities, because of my greed, which is increasing . . . I try to spend quality time with my family and I do spend I hope . . . I spend time with them and I hope they understand at least I hope . . . (Indian man, working for a newspaper)

> It's money, money, money all the time. Money is the most important thing. (Norwegian man, freelancer)

> People are starting to talk a lot about down scaling; it is a hot issue now. They are talking about priorities and putting time above material goods. (Norway, IT designer)

Despite the intrinsic satisfactions and consumerist rewards in much post-industrial work, many of our participants recognise that the 'choice' to work long and hard is always constrained by context (see Lewis, 2003b).

> My concern is that people are working so much and so intensively that everything else gets lost. And people think this is a personal choice. (British woman, researcher)

> These problems are seen as your own fault, it's your choice, and you daren't look because you are then judging yourself too harshly. Before you could blame the system, as was the case with feminism in the 70s, but now you are told and believe there are choices and that it's about the individual. (attendee, international scenario meeting)

---

[5] In the context of the USA, Schor (1998) argues that middle-class Americans are caught in a spiral of spending and regardless of their salaries, need to work long and intensively to meet their rising consumer expectations and standards; see also Layard (2003; 2005), writing in the UK on happiness and economics.

The 'choice' explanation tends to neglect the profound effects of the changing nature of work, employer strategies and certain management practices discussed earlier. It fails to consider persisting organisational constraints and new ways of controlling workers. It also encourages a belief that failure to complete work in a specified time frame, to avoid working extra hours, is a personal inadequacy rather than a problem of excessive work-loads. Many people internalise intensified performance needs and team targets, which can contribute to stress and anxiety, rather than blaming 'norms' and workloads within wider systemic cultures in organisations.

The notion of 'choice' also needs to be unpacked in terms of the impact on other workers.

> I'm at the point in my life where I do work a zillion hours. I always did, it's my per-
> sonality. But people thought if I worked a zillion hours, I couldn't really value someone
> who didn't work a zillion hours. If they got e-mails from me at 3:00 am (which they
> do) or 12:00 at night (which they do), then that meant that they should be sending
> e-mails at 3:00, or that that's what I valued. (American woman, NGO)

The choices of the few can impact negatively on 'choices', well-being and equity experi-enced by the many – even if this is not the intention of the person working long hours.

Hence, what we see is a very complex picture. Excessive workloads can be compelling but also oppressive. They can deplete time, energy and emotional resources for other activities in life (Burchall et al., 2002).

CONSEQUENCES FOR EQUITY, WELL-BEING AND SUSTAINABILITY

The intensification and invasiveness of paid work make it difficult for those with caring commitments to live up to the increasingly demanding 'ideal' associated with full-time work. The tensions that young women, in particular, experience between paid work and family responsibilities are well-documented in academic books, novels and the popular press.[6] However, the notion of the 'ideal' worker also penalises men who may want to be more involved in caring activities. We saw this in the case of Johan, for example, in our Dutch opening story. Despite the initiatives introduced by the Dutch Government to ease the sharing of care between mothers and fathers and his professed willingness to change, he did not feel that it would be possible to alter his working patterns in his organisation.

Thus, intense working patterns and 'ideal' worker assumptions often result in men and women adopting 'traditional' patterns of working and caring, even among couples wanting to be more egalitarian. This, then, reinforces the beliefs of some employers.

> Some industries see work and family as incompatible, which fuels gender inequities.
> There is a suggestion that some couples like to arrange themselves in more 'traditional'
> gender roles; but to what extent is this real choice and a real desire or simple prag-
> matism to certain situations deemed out of your control. (Norway, dual-earner couple)

This also contributes to the perpetuation of the pay gap between men and women (see, for example, Anderson, Forth, Metcalf & Kirby, 2001; Smithson, Lewis, Cooper & Dyer, 2004; Whitehouse, Zetlin & Earnshaw, 2001), which in turn appears to make family

---

[6] See, for example, Franks (1999). For an entertaining novel about the struggles women face see Pearson (2003).

decisions to prioritise men's careers more rational.[7] As a result, in some contexts women work part-time, particularly in The Netherlands and the UK. Yet, even in these countries not all women can afford to do this. In other contexts part-time work is not even an option because of poverty or lack of social supports and benefits.

New working arrangements often require more emotional work, which is frequently performed by women in workplaces and, as Joyce Fletcher (1999) has pointed out, tends to be invisible.[8] Although women may find emotional work satisfying, it can be very demanding and perpetuate inequities.

> People talk about the relationship economy and what they are talking about is the way in which trust is a major issue in organisations. Because the organisations are flat and they are fluid and constantly having to accommodate to change, the requirements on those networks constantly have to be strengthened, built, and re-negotiated under that pressure of change. That requires an intensity of emotional labour, which often ends up being handled by women and often does not get the recognition it deserves. (British woman, journalist)

Global 'efficiency' drives and associated lengthening of working hours, intensive working environments, and the deployment of emotional labour can all impact on people's well-being and have implications for the long-term sustainability of individuals, families, communities and of workplace organisations that rely on their human resources (see Galinsky et al., 2001; Sparks et al., 1997; Worrall & Cooper, 2001; Zuzanek, 2005).

> There is a lot of burn-out, resentment, dissatisfaction, and it, it has to come out, it comes out and it's happening. Depression has come into India also now in a big way. A lot of our mental health issues are now coming out in the open, and the worst is that we don't have . . . we still have this taboo against psychiatrists. (Indian woman academic)

> [Depression] is on the rise. It is like catching flu, it is that common . . . this is another crisis that might force us to stop and rethink. (Japanese woman professional)

> . . . some groups of people are working very long hours and they stay at work all day and all night and then we also have this big explosion of long sick leaves because people are stressed out. (Norwegian man, designer)

> There are high rates of people taking early retirement because of disability. Often this is because of mental rather than physical illness, usually attributed to stress, including among young people in their thirties. The government is concerned to address stress and burn-out issues to revert this trend. (attendee, The Netherlands, country meeting)

POLICY IS NOT ENOUGH – IMPLEMENTATION GAPS

Current received wisdom is that it is up to individuals to make changes in their lives or that policies can make a difference. Changes in individual's mindsets and orientations can be an important impetus for changing their own working practices and can perhaps con-

---

[7] See Lister (2003, p. 182), who succinctly argues that: 'a culture of long, paid working hours can serve to constrain male participation in unpaid caring and domestic work, while it also creates barriers to women's full integration and advancement in the workplace, thereby fuelling the viscous circle created by the sexual division of labour'.

[8] See also Rapoport et al., (2002, pp. 32–35), who discuss notions of competency and ways in which 'feminine' interpersonal skills (which can often be seen as personal attributes rather than something that is learnt and developed) are increasingly sought after but not considered 'real' work. When push comes to shove, technical skills are valued more despite the critical need for both.

tribute to wider organisational change. However, there is a limit to what can be achieved by individual reappraisals and negotiations and not all employees have the capacity or confidence for this. Widespread change requires challenging existing working practices, structures and cultures at a collective and systemic level.

The changing nature of paid work and the composition of the workforce have not been totally lost on governments or workplace organisations. As we discussed in Chapter 2, government and workplace policies have emerged in various combinations in the seven different countries, aiming to enable workers to manage commitments and responsibilities outside of paid work. Both government and workplace policy developments are crucial, and government policies in particular for low paid or vulnerable workers. However, different kinds of policies can have different effects on equity between men and women. For example, longer periods of parental leave, often taken by women, can contribute to women's subsequent marginalisation in paid work as they can reduce human capital or networking opportunities (see Devon & Moss, 2002). Developing affordable and accessible childcare services is important too, although this can simply encourage more women to enter paid work without encouraging men to change their behaviour or employers and managers to change their expectations. In this case, women experience pressures and responsibilities beyond the workplace resulting in the often discussed second shift (Hochschild with Machung, 1989). So policies in themselves, while offering vital practical support, are rarely sufficient in themselves to bring about equitable and sustainable solutions. Gaps between policies – no matter how well meaning and intended – and practice persist. In short, policies do little to challenge 'ideal' worker assumptions or workplace structures, cultures and practices and, while offering some compensation to or support for women, can reflect and exacerbate assumptions about men and women's roles and inequities between them.[9]

In Norway, the country in our study with the most progressive government policies – including subsidised childcare, generous parental leave and active measures to encourage men to participate more in family life – men and women have a relatively high sense of entitlement to measures that enable them to harmonise paid work with other parts of life in ways that are equitable (Lewis & Smithson, 2001). Even there, however, demanding workloads and 'ideal' worker norms, particularly in highly competitive workplaces, often reduce men's willingness to take-up their entitlements (Brandth & Kvande, 2001). In The Netherlands, flexible parental leave rights enable a growing minority of fathers to reduce their working hours when their children are young. Again, however, as discussed in Chapter 2, this is not possible in all workplaces and it is more common in the public sector. Workplace norms and practices often undermine government initiatives.

Government policies can also be undermined by the outsourcing of work from many 'developed' to 'developing' countries with poorer conditions and protection. Unless international standards are put in place this may make any policies to support the reconciliation or harmonisation of paid work with other parts of life increasingly difficult to maintain, or even irrelevant, as competition between countries increases.

---

[9] See Daly and Rake (2003) for a thorough analysis and account of many gender inequities both mitigated and exacerbated in the context of particular welfare state arrangements in eight different countries (France, Germany, Ireland, Italy, The Netherlands, Sweden, the UK and the USA). In terms of challenging 'ideal' worker assumptions, an interesting development has occurred in Sweden. In recognition of the ways in which employees taking leaves can be penalised, legislation has been introduced banning those using parental leave from workplace discrimination (see Gauthier, 2005). However, it remains to be seen what legislation can do without wider cultural changes in workplaces.

Organisational policies and initiatives have also emerged to varying degrees within all the countries in our study, either as a complement to government initiatives or as an alternative in the absence of government supports. In the absence of regulation, voluntary employer initiatives are often encouraged by promoting a 'business case' argument. Employers are encouraged to develop policies, such as flexible working arrangements, to aid recruitment and retention or sometimes to better reflect the diversity of the organisation's customers or clients. There is much discussion of win-win solutions but the business case tends to imply that it is the employers' wins that are prioritised (Harker & Lewis, 2001). As with government initiatives there is also a widespread gap between policy and practice. Workplace policies are often poorly communicated to employees and tend to be largely regarded as policies for women, or at least for those that do not wish to conform to standard working times. Those using such policy provisions are often regarded as 'non-ideal' workers and marginalised as a result. Moreover, the common practice of outsourcing much work to freelancers or agencies can be used to absolve employers from the need to provide these rights except to a core, skilled workforce. Furthermore, not all workplaces accept the business case, so in the absence of government regulation, access to even the most basic forms of policies or benefits is uneven.

BEYOND QUICK FIXES TOWARDS SYSTEMIC CHANGE

Formal employer policies can be regarded as quick fixes. They tend to introduce change around the margins to enable employees with non-work commitments to retain links with employment. However, they fail to challenge or systemically alter organisational structures and cultures: values and assumptions that determine and reflect current social constructions of 'ideal' workers. Moreover, as one of our participants from the UK suggests, to have such initiatives in place can be worse than doing nothing as it paints an illusion of support within a penalising culture.

> It's got to be systemic change or nothing. I do think that with these things, if they are not like that, then they are worse than nothing . . . if you want to have work–life balance initiatives but people will still be punished for using these, then it is easier before when people just knew where they stood, even if it is six feet under. For it to work, it has to be sincere. (British man, researcher)

Illusions of support can emerge and problems subsequently experienced are internalised as individual failings (see Coppock, Haydon & Richter, 1995). Persisting structures, cultures and practices can undermine effectiveness as well as equity (Rapoport et al., 2002). We illustrate the problems of policies without widespread systemic change by returning to our Norwegian characters Per and Siri from our opening stories. Many similar stories can be found in other countries.

> There are provisions for flexible working arrangements in Per and Siri's workplace. In many departments, men and women are encouraged to make use of them. After talking with his wife, Siri, Per approaches his employer about working three days a week. He is prepared to take a slight drop in salary and his boss agrees reluctantly. For six months it works well. He has more time and energy to give to his family, personal and business relationships. He works in an international section and is now more willing to leave his mobile phone on and take work-related calls as and when they come up. But over time his boss feels increasingly uncomfortable with the situation. Despite the Norwegian political ideology of supporting fathers in modifying paid work for

family reasons, Per's boss is not used to having such a senior member of his team away from the office and dislikes having to plan meetings to suit Per's schedule. After seven months Per receives a call to say if he wants to retain the hours he is doing, he should move to a different lower status job. Per is very frustrated and after much discussion with his boss and deliberation with Siri, he makes a decision to leave and go freelance.

It was not only Per who lost out in this example. His international contacts and knowledge made him a valuable member of the team. Without his input, his company no longer benefited from his contacts and widespread experience.

In this chapter we have argued that:

- The ideal worker is still widely viewed as someone who does not let family or other commitments interfere with paid work.
- Assumptions about ideal workers are exacerbated in the context of global economic competitiveness.
- Paid work, for many people, invades all other parts of life.
- The invasiveness of work and assumptions about ideal workers has consequences for equity, well-being and human sustainability.
- Current received wisdom is that it is up to individuals to make changes in their lives or that policies can make a difference. But widespread change also requires challenging existing working practices, structures and cultures at a collective level.

To conclude, we argue that the ways that *commitment* is defined in current forms of *capitalism* along with growing *consumerism* can undermine the value of *care* and experiences of *connectedness*. The focus on 'quick fixes', profit, 'efficiency' and productivity instead of – rather than alongside – individual and social needs is not sustainable in the long term. The challenge for the future is to think about the ways in which paid work interacts with and can be enhanced by people's experiences at multiple levels of society: including individual experiences, as well as families, communities and wider societies more generally.

The next chapter explores experiences of care and connectedness in families, friendships and communities in the context of increasingly invasive paid work.

CHAPTER 5

Care and Connections: Families, Communities, Friendships and Care of the Self

Paid work can be an important source of connection, pleasure, identity and purpose. Yet, for both men and women, pleasure, identity and purpose can also come from unpaid work, care and connectedness in families, friendship networks and communities. People need, and benefit from, connections with others across a range of life experiences. However, the current invasiveness of paid work impacts on activities and experiences in all other areas of life.

Of course aspects of care and connectedness, like aspects of work, can be double-edged. In some circumstances work – whether it is paid or unpaid – can be experienced as drudgery and be undervalued. Forms of connectedness can be both satisfying and oppressive. For example, constant connectedness via access to technology such as email can be positive or can make it hard for people to switch off from paid work. The sense of obligation to provide unpaid care for family or friends can be both rewarding and burdensome.

We use care in the broadest sense: as an integral part of everything people do in life, as an activity and a feeling, and as a central part of our reflections on harmonising paid work with other parts of life. Connectedness – and care – is something that occurs across a range of life experiences. Janet Fink (2004, p. 27) argues that 'there has been a shift from conceptualising care as being simply based in networks of family and kin relation-ships to an acknowledgement that care relations connect people throughout society'. Here, care and connectedness are used to reflect the myriad of reciprocal ways in which people can care for and connect with others: within interpersonal relationships between men and women; in families; in friendships; in communities; and in workplaces.[1] This understand-ing of care is based on an idea of interdependence, interconnectedness and awareness that the vast majority of people are dependent, whether they realise it or not, on the care, attention and respect of others (see Sevenhuijsen, 1998; Tronto, 1993; Williams, 2001; Williams, 2004). In this chapter we illustrate how people's experiences of care and con-nectedness in families, communities and friendships are changing in the context of the

---

[1] Tronto (1993, p. 10) argues that care is 'a species activity that includes everything we do to maintain, continue and repair our "world" so that we can live in it as well as possible. That world includes our bodies, ourselves, and our environment, all of which we seek to interweave in a complex, life-sustaining web.'

current invasiveness of paid work. We explore this using our data from the seven countries at this point of social and economic evolution.

CARE AND CONNECTEDNESS

Families

There are both negative and positive aspects of changes in family life in relation to paid work experiences (see Jamieson, 1998; Williams, 2004). The negative view of family change is that families are less stable and more fragmented than in the past, and in selfish individualist decline. It is argued that the demands of contemporary workplaces can be at odds with values required to maintain family and personal life (Bauman, 2003; Sennett, 1998), thus reflecting connections with trends in paid work. A more positive view is that family change reflects greater freedom of choice and opportunities for people to shape their own lives and develop more rewarding relationships. For example, increased opportunities for women in paid work have somewhat democratised personal relationships and given women more options (Giddens, 1992; 1999). In reality, the picture is far more complex. For example, relationships between men and women are changing but many inequities persist.[2]

Some of our opening stories illustrate these complexities in 'developed' and 'developing' countries. Anna, from The Netherlands, benefits from a fairly egalitarian relationship with her husband Johan and meaningful paid work, but finds that increased pressures and workloads also affect her experiences of paid work and time for her family in negative ways. Ravi, from India, has really benefited from opportunities to work in a multinational company. Yet he is torn between his desires to increase the material standard of living and opportunities for his children, and his sense of obligation and desire to take time away from work to care for his elderly mother back in the village where he grew up.

It is not only industrialised or post-industrialised countries or contexts that are experiencing the changing impact of paid work on family and kinships. Urbanisation and rising participation in formal labour markets in most of the world's 'developing' countries, as well as 'efficiency' transformations of agricultural economies that can pull spheres of work and family apart, dramatically change the ways in which parents, children and other family members can care and be cared for. Jody Heymann and colleagues argue that working families in 'developing' countries are now facing similar dilemmas to families in industrialised nations about how to harmonise paid work with other parts of life, but that their problems are compounded by significantly higher care giving burdens and far fewer resources (Heymann et al., 2004).[3]

There is much talk, in all the countries in our study, of changes in family structures or what is sometimes described as the 'breakdown' of the family, often in the context of the

---

[2] Williams (2004, pp. 21–23) gives a number of examples including the fact that there has always been some degree of family diversity as well as inequalities between different families; that there have always been children born out of wedlock but that in earlier times this was kept more hidden; that divorce in itself does not always lead to child anxiety but depends on the processes through which some adults and children are able to negotiate change better than others; and that although many women have more freedom, domestic violence continues to be endemic. She notes 'it is the unevenness of change, where old practices jostle with new ideals of equality between men and women which, some say, gives rise to the necessity for continual negotiation between couples or between parents and children' (p. 22).

invasiveness of paid work. For example, there is much discussion of changes and continuities in the incidence of extended kin relations living with or in close proximity to each other, particularly in India. Extended families in India have enabled some family members to work more intensely or extensively. But these families are now often breaking down in the context of rising incomes and financial resources that can make it necessary or possible to live in multiple households.

> The big cities are putting pressure [on] . . . the joint family system because the houses are becoming smaller and parents do not want to relocate from smaller towns to big towns because the quality of life is not really as good as in the small towns, you have a large house and a large place and large garden where you can roam. Well you can't do that in an apartment . . . so from that perspective the joint family . . . where the grandparents and the parents and the kids live together . . . it is already not happening in the big cities and towns (Indian man, manager)

Some people experience this trend very positively, while others regret it not only because of the impact on family relations but also because it is believed that extended families teach skills that are important in the workplace.

> I regret the decline of joint families and the growth of nuclear families in urban areas. The joint family system teaches people to make sacrifices. Those who have come from joint families can make sacrifices and work better in teams. People from small nuclear families find it harder to work in teams. In joint families, you see more of people's weaknesses but still love them and so you develop tolerance. (Indian entrepreneur, male)

Nevertheless, there is also debate about the nature of this trend. Some of our Indian participants believe that the numbers of joint families may be growing again as people realise that the presence of more kin can support harmonising paid work with caring responsibilities, whether caring for children or the elderly. However, we also hear that nuclear families can be threatened in India with rising divorce among affluent dual-earner nuclear families.

Participants in all the countries talk about the impact of extreme work involvement on family relationships, whether this is because of employer demands, career pressures, to fight for a 'cause' or for other reasons.

> I was a trade unionist, which was a rough environment, we were dealing with hard issues of exploitation, and we ignored the home. My first marriage broke down, because of many contributing factors. Thank god we are friends, but we are still a broken family. At that time, because I was driven by the struggle and the need to participate and end apartheid . . . I gave my absolute all to it . . . a lot of marriages broke up. (South African man, trade unionist)

> So many couples have become divorced because they have been so involved with their careers and have been so involved in feeling many of the issues associated with this that they are not friends anymore. They do not enjoy themselves, they do not enjoy

---

[3] See also Aryee (2005) writing on work–family challenges in the Sub-Saharan African context. In particular, he notes that extended family ties are strong, nursing homes for the elderly remain foreign concepts, having large numbers of children is the norm, and an absence of modern household conveniences all compound time and energy required for family and domestic obligations and responsibilities. Rapid urbanisation has also put strains on electricity and water supplies, which further increases the time and energy required for domestic tasks. At the same time, job insecurity in the context of high unemployment has increased the amount of time employees spend in the workplace or that others spend in income-generating activities. However, as this is often seen as time away for the family rather than time away from the family, he finds inadequate pay is a stronger factor of work–family conflict than in 'developed' contexts.

> love and romance and it is just like being puppets on strings. People are so concerned
> about being perfect and successful. They want to have it all, but you can never do this
> and you have to find out what are the most important things. (Norway, woman manager)

Extreme pressures can also impact on children – not because both parents are working, but because, as Ellen Galinsky notes in the US context, parents are so 'wired' when they come home from intensive and demanding paid work (Galinsky, 1998).

Thus, the invasiveness of paid work can contribute to family break-ups and care can take place in increasingly diverse circumstances.[4] Trends, such as the rise in lone parent-hood, or elderly parents caring for grandchildren because their own children have died of HIV/AIDS in South Africa, for example, make it difficult for people in many diverse cir-cumstances to conform to 'ideal' worker assumptions at the same time as caring for family members. Failure of workplaces to accommodate people with diverse family and personal responsibilities can thus also contribute to poverty in many families in 'developed' and 'developing' countries.[5] This, in turn, can impact strongly on experiences of care and connection.

While trends and links are tenuous, extreme involvement in formal paid work can not only contribute towards the breakdown of relationships: it can also make it difficult to make connections and establish relationships in the first place.

> People increasingly form relationships through the internet because they are always
> working. But there is not enough time to develop relationships and they are often short
> term and casual. The loss of time people have for each other is also leading to a lot of
> affairs and relationship breakdown: communication, including emails and texts, enables
> affairs to be discovered more easily. (Japanese woman, researcher)

Communities

Other forms of care and connectedness are in the community. Yet changes in the nature of paid work and family and kinship relationships all contribute to the difficulties of defin-ing what is actually meant by 'community'. There are communities of work, communit-ies of interests, neighbourhood communities, and virtual or global communities.[6] Cultures of overwork can make it difficult to participate in communities, however defined. More-over, the relocation of jobs to other countries or the changing nature of paid work in par-ticular societies, such as the closure of coal mines in the UK, can undermine sustainable communities.[7] Yet connectedness in communities is all the more necessary in the context of both overwork and under-work.

Communities offer an important source of formal and informal support for the har-monisation of paid work with caring needs and commitments (Hertz & Ferguson, 1998;

---

[4] There have been many changes in families and households, such as the growth of lone parent families, same sex couples, reconstituted families which involve divorced couples often with children remarrying, and increasing numbers of people living alone. (See Lewis, Kiernan & Land, 1998; Kamerman & Kahn, 1997).

[5] Poverty amongst women with no or limited access to paid work can often occur when women have to head households. At the same time, unequal household distribution of resources can also mean women in male headed households can experience hidden poverty. See, for example, Daly, 1992; Daly & Rake, 2003; Pahl, 1989; see also Lewis et al., 2000, who discuss the ways in which unpaid carers are often excluded from anything other than very low paid and insecure work.

[6] See, for example, Poarch (1998) for a discussion on the workplace as a source of community.

[7] See, for example, Winsom and Leach (2002), who recount experiences of communities in rural Ontario, Canada, following the relocation of manufacturing companies. They find that while attachment to rural communities can sustain people through difficult times, such as factory closures, it can also condemn those reluctant to move to the cities to contingent and unstable work.

Kagan, Lewis & Heaton, 1999). In a formal capacity, home helps, community nurses, or people working in a variety of care institutions all provide vital services. Yet, as they are participating in paid work, they are also exposed to many of the pressures we discussed in Chapter 4. Care workers are often low paid and new public management structures and incentives contribute to overload and pressure. It also contributes to high levels of staff turnover, which can impact on the care received by clients (see Fink, 2004). In informal capacities, neighbours and support groups can also provide much support in the practical and emotional difficulties in combining paid work with other parts of life. Community or civic participation are also important sites for promoting inclusion for collective participation and influence of democratic processes, and for developing skills that are relevant in workplaces and families.[8]

Robert Putnam (2000) has argued that people have become increasingly disconnected from one another and their communities beyond paid work largely as a consequence of the invasiveness of paid work.[9] People have less time to participate in religious institutions, school governing bodies and teacher-parent activities, political activities and for general volunteering in community programmes. Ann Bookman (2004) agrees that workplace cultures and expectations often reduce the amount of time people have to contribute to or participate in their communities beyond paid work, but argues that many people are forging new community links to buffer the difficulties of harmonising work with other parts of life (Bookman, 2004). Both Putnam and Bookman are writing in the USA but in our study we find support for both views in all the other countries. There is concern about the decline of community ties. For example, a Japanese woman says:

> During our high period of economic growth lots of people lost interest in the community. We feel the community is now vacant and this means children's delinquency and that they are not being looked after . . . We are calling for people to spend some time in the community and to re-establish their networks. It's being discussed a lot. But the need is being felt keenly, rather than it is happening. (Japanese woman, government advisor)

There is also evidence of new community actions and initiatives developing to support the harmonisations of multiple parts of life. For example:

> In KwaZulu-Natal we are launching a programme on HIV and AIDS education. In the process of training, we came across these girls who had dropped out, not in school because of a variety of reasons, and they are helping people within the communities, the children who are sick, children who don't have parents; the pensioners, taking them to the hospitals, and so on . . . so we are trying to help them. (South Africa, NGO woman worker)

Friendships

With work, family and community relationships in a state of flux, many of our participants emphasise the importance of friendship as a crucial way in which to feel cared for and connected with others. 'Life deals nasty blows and if you haven't got those factors

---

[8] One example here comes from Kofman, Phyizacklea, Raghuram and Sales (2000), who discuss the ways in which migrant women can often be used as cultural mediators between migrant communities and welfare workers or local authorities.
[9] See also a report by the OECD (1997) that recognises the impacts of working times and current ways of working on the ways in which people organise their lives and ways in which societies and communities function.

that help you handle these, such as good friends, you are more vulnerable' (British woman, trade union).

Like family and community, friendship is difficult to define.[10] Some of our participants make a distinction between friendships and other forms of connectedness. Others are unclear about the nature of many of their relationships as boundaries between work, family and community become increasingly blurred. 'My friends are people I interact with. Personally I really no longer really have a friend. I belong to a big family; I meet with people at the workplace, the church. So these people I meet with are my friends' (South African man, trade unionist).

Yet, many others feel that friendship is a casualty of the invasiveness of paid work.[11]

> Friends? I don't know if I have any? Do I have any real friends? (US woman, researcher)

> If you are working and engaged with the family in a more hands on way there is less time for friendships. I have a joke, that I can't 'do' friends anymore, but it's not a joke. By the time I have handled my work, which I love, and the kids, whom I love, and spent some time with my partner, whom I love, and done the necessary domestic work, there is no real time for friends . . . Friends are not high up in my priorities. (British man, freelance writer)

> Friendship is a low priority for many people. Either work or family comes first, and then the other. And friendship suffers the most. That has been the cost. (Norwegian man, trades union)

> I think people are more and more disconnected because they are just too busy. There is not enough time. I hear everybody say that they don't have enough time to meet our friends . . . we don't have enough time to be with our old girlfriends. (Norwegian woman, administrator)

> I do have friends, but hardly any. I am in the office at weekends. That is my life. I have found my work environment is my second home, even Sundays. I haven't been to church this year. (South African woman, NGO worker)

Total involvement in paid work can make the workplace a crucial site for friendship (Poarch, 1998). This can be very positive.

> I think we have to be more honest about the fact that when we say we don't have friends, what we mean is that we don't have non-work friends. People tend to think it is wrong to make all your friends at work, but I don't think it is . . . and in non-white collar work, why is it that dinner ladies and sewer workers report to be the most satisfied at work? It's not the money, but the community or clubs, in a sense, in which you belong to. (British man, researcher)

In other contexts, work-related friendships are regarded as more problematic: '. . . relationships at work [are] diluting and diluting very fast . . . friendships and relationships at work are very superficial . . . maybe one or two people you can really call friends at work. Otherwise it is vanishing' (Indian country meeting).

There is also some discussion of friendships as temporary and 'disposable' in modern life. 'We are getting better at disposable friendships . . .' (British man, journalist). Devel-

---

[10] See Pahl (2000), who explores the contested nature and meaning of friendship in historical and contemporary contexts.

[11] A similar conclusion was drawn in a qualitative research project of middle managers in Australia (see Parris, Vickers & Wilkes, 2005). Parris et al. note that the demands of their working lives had a significant effect on their friendships. Respondents spoke of friends as a vital source and protection of individual well-being yet friendship can be a first casualty of intensive workplace demands.

opments in technology, despite making it easier for work to intrude into private life also enable people to keep up with friends in their busy lives, although some feel this is no substitute for face-to-face connections.

> I'm not terribly good at keeping up with friends because I haven't got time. But nowadays, with the internet it's getting easier. (Japanese woman, civil servant)

> Real friendships are based on real conversations, which you can't have with email, so you have to make space for them. (British man, journalist)

There are other ways of sustaining friendships. For example, some people suggest that although they may have less time in their lives at particular moments, friends often understand and are in a similar position. It is thought that these relationships can be reactivated at later periods.

> My friends are incredibly important to me. All of us recognise the complexities of our lives, we have all got small children and those are friendships that will last, we may see each other only every six months but they are all there and when we have more time we will be able to reactivate them. (British woman, author)

However, friendship was a surprisingly sensitive topic in many of our conversations in the different countries. People who had talked freely and expansively about their paid work and families were often reluctant to talk about friends and the conversation turned to loneliness on many occasions. Discussions about friendships were often emotionally charged either because of the significant role friends play, or the uneasiness about discussing a neglected area of life.

LONELINESS AND DISCONNECTION

We hear much concern in countries in our study about not having invested sufficiently in friendships and other forms of connectedness. This contributes to a sense of loneliness expressed by some people in all countries. For example: 'What I see is this distributed work, this distributed friendship, basically an increasingly atomised world, and I think people are all feeling increasingly lonely. Everybody needs community' (British man, business commentator). This is widely attributed, directly or indirectly, to the invasiveness of paid work and consumerism.

> Loneliness seems to me a big subject because we have invested an enormous amount in the material improvement of lives. We have tried to improve the human condition away from nasty, brutish and short and what I think we have failed to appreciate is how we are driving towards lives that are long, lonely and anxious. The length of life is no determinant of the quality or the happiness or anything and it's a bizarre sort of focus really. It's the richness and the dignity of the life that matters. We've misunderstood that. The length and the material comfort is what we have been pre-occupied with. (British woman, author)

This sense of loneliness and disconnection can exacerbate further the invasiveness of paid work. If people are busy working, they do not have to think about a lack of other forms of connectedness or difficult or absent relationships in their lives.

> earlier I had a relationship with my mother and now . . . the relationship has become different . . . the workplace is unfriendly, friends are so busy that if I have the time they don't have the time . . . and my sisters . . . with whom I had relationships, they are in different stages of their lifecycles . . . suddenly in my own Delhi . . . I feel kind of alienated . . . I have my husband [but] we do talk but not as much as I'd like to . . . so I'm

> feeling kind of lonely here which may be happening to others and therefore they start concentrating on their work so much . . . Yes, I find myself telling myself that, if there is nothing else, you put all your energies in your work and draw your pleasures from work. (Indian woman, teacher)

> No one is talking about the crisis of meaning in mainstream adult life, which connects with sex and sexuality in and outside of marriage, parenting, caring for elders, social responsibility, the meaning of work and essentially what we are all actually working for. I think one of the main reasons we allow work to be so invasive is that it's an escape from and easier to handle than all these aspects of the crisis in adult life. (American woman, NGO)

Being able to draw pleasure and meaning from paid work may be a sustainable strategy in the short term. However, many recognise that this could be a problem in retirement, or in other periods when paid work no longer fills up so much of their time.

> Friendships are very important, but I'm not sure if I have invested sufficiently in them, and invested sufficiently for later years. There is a scarcity of time for friends . . . but that will change, and maybe that is why I am hesitating about retirement. (Dutch woman, consultant)

> Young men are looking at their fathers who have devoted their lives to their work and then when they retire they lose touch with their friends because they have cultivated them through their workplace and when they retire that is the end of it. (Japanese woman, researcher)

CONSEQUENCES FOR EQUITY, WELL-BEING AND SUSTAINABILITY

Changes in families, communities and friendships and the loneliness and disconnectedness that can be linked with the invasiveness of paid work have important implications for equity, well-being and sustainability.

Equity

As we discussed in Chapter 4, when paid work is very demanding, it is often impossible for more than one household member to conform to 'ideal' worker expectations. This creates obvious problems for lone parents, and in dual-earner households it is usually women who reduce their involvement in paid work or take on a double burden of paid work with care of children and/or of the elderly. It is much more difficult for men to do so. This is partly because men's higher earnings make it appear a more rational decision for women rather than men to cut down on work. However, it is also because of assumptions about separate spheres, in which women are assumed to be the main carers. The 'ideal' mother is still widely regarded as someone who puts unpaid care before paid work: the antithesis of the 'ideal' worker (Lewis, 1991).[12] Despite the media myth of 'post-

---

[12] See also Knijn (2000), who gives a lucid account of the ways in which 'ideal' mother assumptions came into recent ascendancy. She notes that with the emergence of modern domestic appliances during the 1950s and 1960s, housekeeping became less time-consuming. However, at the same time, Knijn notes that mothering became more intensive citing the influence of John Bowlby and others stressing the importance of maternal attachment and the mother as the pivotal care giver creating nurturing, safe, loving environment for children to develop in. Thus, the time saved by housework went into increasingly intensive mothering. But many contemporary shifts again challenge this. Giving care presumes time, proximity and willingness – all of which are under pressure. Women have been described as a reserve army of carers, to be brought in whenever there is a crisis (see, for example, Dalley, 1996; Lewis et al., 2000).

feminism' in many western contexts, social pressures for women to care remain pervasive. Meanwhile, new family and employment dilemmas loom for the future in the context of ageing populations, growing care needs and the spiralling greed of workplaces in the post-industrial economy.

The increasingly demanding nature of paid work, alongside assumptions and contemporary realities that women tend to be more involved with unpaid care, thus contributes to inequities between men and women. Yet, it also contributes to inequities between different women within and across different countries. The use of nannies and maids among affluent families in the 'developed' and some 'developing' countries such as India, enable men and women in dual-earner and some extended families to conform to long and intensive working hours. This leaves serious problems of harmonising paid work with other parts of life for domestic workers themselves, who have often migrated from other less affluent contexts or countries: 'most of [the domestic workers] tend to be migrants . . . in Delhi you will find a lot of people from the hills . . . they work over here and their families are left behind and they therefore have to deal with that issue' (Indian man, hotel manager).

Issues of harmonising paid work with other parts of life are not only globally experienced, but sometimes globally connected, in what Barbara Ehrenreich and Arlie Hochschild (2003) describe as a global care chain. Poverty pushes many migrant women away from their families while care deficits in 'developed' countries pull them into other families. This was seen in our US story in the case of Enrika, Elizabeth's nanny from the Philippines, who enabled Elizabeth to work long hours. The global care chain, according to Ehrenreich and Hochschild results from multiple factors: the failure of some governments in 'developed' countries to provide adequate care supports; the complacency of some governments in 'developing' countries who benefit from the money these women send back; and the lack of change in many men's behaviour in 'developed' and 'developing' countries. This global care chain is also sustained by the changing nature of work and demands of employers in the context of global competitive capitalism.

Well-being

Lack of time for connecting can create extra pressures and also impact on well-being. People can expect too much from single relationships. For example, a lack of time and energy for connecting with friends and others can contribute to strain in intimate relationships.

> Romantic relationships are starting to become more like friendships. The desire for friendship is being distilled into our romantic relationships, which is not unproblematic. I certainly feel it with my partner; we're business partners, co-parents, lovers, friends and housemates. So the amount of strain, as everything gets poured in, especially if they die, or with the rising divorce rates and break up escalates. (British man, researcher)

> You can get into some big trouble, because you don't have a network. You are too dependent on very few people and that relationship with your wife or family may suffer from the situation where you work too much and then to have that as the only way of getting help, that's really very difficult. (Norwegian man, teacher)

At the same time, increasing family diversity, including break-ups and the forging of new relationships can also result in people's family networks and obligations being more complicated and dispersed and so requiring more time and energy.[13]

The intensification of paid work, together with rising expectations of parenthood and the importance of parental involvement for children's development and life chances,[14] can also contribute to the strain and pressure of combining paid work with childcare. As Rosenfeld and Wise (2000, p. 202), writing in the US context, put it: 'working to be the best parents we can be, we run and run . . . we are drowning in car pools and crowded calendars, trapped by high expectations and escalating standards . . . dual-income families are . . . characterised as being overextended, overworked, overwhelmed and over the top.' Expectations in paid work *and* in family life can contribute to a sense of general life intensification, but these expectations can also further exacerbate depleting networks of care and connection.

> Mothers and fathers feel compelled to spend so much time with their children. So we see intensification of work and of parenthood, and this means you are abandoning friendships and communities. (British woman, researcher)

As people live longer, grandparents can be an important source of care providers for young children, although if they are in paid work themselves, this can create further pressures and tensions in the context of harmonising paid work with other aspects of life. However, demands of care of the elderly are also intensifying and some of our participants feel overwhelmed. This care is identified as a major concern for the future in all the countries.

> I have to care for my mother, who lives miles away from where I live and work, which is stressful. I have to take the bus, which takes hours, and it is taking a hell of a lot out of me. My extended family is making tremendous demands on me. (South African woman, NGO)

> Caring for older parents . . . that is coming up yes, it is going to be a very big issue in India in the coming years because the bulk of the population so far has been young, the lifespan is rising, the population is ageing but not as fast as it is in the West, but there is virtually no social security for the old here . . . and so far the only security was the family, you live with your son or daughter . . . but with the nuclear family coming in and the extended family dying out that has become more and more difficult, and city life and urban people will find it very difficult, so this is going to be a very big issue (Indian man, senior manager)

Care of the elderly is a particular problem in India where there is 'virtually no social security' as mentioned in one of the quotes above. However, in a climate of family diversity and welfare pressures or cutbacks in other countries, there is much generic concern about how this care will be managed in the future.[15]

---

[13] See Williams, 2004. See also Barolsky (2003), who discusses the 'over-extended family' in the South African context as people have to care for family members and others in their community who have lost significant others through the HIV/AIDS epidemic.

[14] See for example Esping-Andersen (2002), who discusses the importance of quality parenthood for the child's future life chances particularly in the context of working towards fairer societies. More generally, in the context of people working often long hours in paid work, parents can feel guilty about the lack of actual time (quantity) they spend with their children and when this is the case may try to make this up with more 'quality' time. See also Lister (2004), who discusses the danger of focusing on children's life chances if it places too much instrumental emphasis on children as future citizen workers rather than children who deserve a childhood in its own right.

[15] See for example Royal Commission on Long Term Care (1999); Myles (2002), for a succinct summary of elder care and pension dilemmas; and for critical accounts that argue elder care is less of a burden than often portrayed, see Wilson (2000) or Phillipson (1996).

In the context of what we hear about disconnections from wider support networks and a fragile sense of community, the implications of the intensification of both work and care for individuals, families and in communities can be immense. Against this backdrop, time for leisure and care of the self is vital, yet also under threat.

> I see a lot of mental, emotional overload because there is just too much going on. People don't have time to just sit down and be. (Norwegian woman, administrator)

As work becomes more invasive, and for many people more compelling, the boundaries between work and leisure often become blurred.[16] As we discussed in Chapter 4, some people say paid work is what they enjoy doing, but many acknowledge it stops them doing other things.

> I have desperately been trying to learn to relearn to play the piano for the last year . . . and I need to spend half an hour a day, but whenever given a choice, work will predominate, and I let that happen. (British woman, working in an NGO)

This woman perceives this as something she *lets* happen. Given a choice, she will *allow* work to predominate. Like many of our other participants in different countries, she berates herself for her lack of 'self-control' and underestimates workplace constraints and expectations that may affect such a 'choice'.

It is not only paid work itself but also work mentality that spills over into people's relationships and leisure (Bauman, 2003). As people are encouraged to keep fit, take part in sport or take up hobbies, or engage in enjoyable activities beyond work, leisure has also become something that people are expected to do. Leisure becomes another demand that 'ought' to be satisfied, often in addition to, rather than in place of, aspects of paid and unpaid work. This exacerbates the sense of busyness. There are cultural differences in the valuing of time for hobbies and leisure. For example:

> There is a tradition of hobbies, of introducing yourself by saying what hobbies you have [in Japan]. It is expected. Some people will say flower arranging, others will say hiking. I do pottery at the weekends, and I write poems and go to poetry classes twice a month and have friends there. I haven't really got time, but I make it, I need to . . . I steal time. (Japanese woman, government advisor)

Nevertheless in this example, although hobbies are highly valued, this Japanese woman talks about having to 'steal time', thus reflecting another pressure.

In cultures of busyness, where notions of the effective use of time and productivity and efficiency in the workplace permeate into all areas of our lives, leisure can too easily be experienced as non-productive, or a waste of time. As the intensification of work makes it increasingly difficult to switch from the language and mindsets of paid work, many people we have spoken with say they do not know what to do with 'spare time'.

People who do make time for leisure, however, discuss the benefits this brings for both paid work and their personal well-being. A Norwegian government official, for example, speaks about her passion for golf. She says it enables her to clear her head, which means she can return to her paid work and operate more productively afterwards getting tasks done in much less time.

---

[16] Leisure, like other concepts discussed in this chapter, is difficult to define, and particularly so in the context of the shifting boundaries between work, families, communities and friendships. Leisure is often defined as the antithesis of work and is seen as non-obligated time or activities that are freely chosen, even a relief from work. But definitions of leisure in terms of free time have proved problematic (Haworth & Veal, 2005). As post-industrial work, especially knowledge work becomes more satisfying and even addictive, it is what many people choose to do with much of their time, although this must be considered within contextual constraints (see Lewis, 2003b).

> Golf is particularly good for me . . . at the first hole my head is still full of work and I
> don't focus on the ball, but by the second I focus and my head has cleared. After the
> golf I go back and do another couple of hours work, thinking more clearly. The work
> I do after playing golf is much more useful. I do much more in that hour than if I
> had been sitting there all the time and had not played golf. It also helps me sleep.
> (Norwegian woman, government official)

Leisure is an important way of relaxing and refreshing the spirit. It is an important
dimension of caring for the self and can enhance and sustain well-being and performance
in all spheres of life. It is also a channel for obtaining gratification from working at something that is unpaid.

Sustainability

As Madeleine Bunting (2004, p. xxi) points out, 'just as the late twentieth century grasped
the fact that there was a crisis of environmental sustainability, the twenty first century is
beginning to grasp the dimensions of a comparable crisis, this time of human sustainability – a scarcity of conditions which nurture resilient, secure individuals, families, friendships, and communities. Who has time to care for whom in the overwork culture?'

The lack of time and energy for care and connectedness and for care of the self, because
of the demands of paid work, can impact negatively on the sustainability of individuals
and of human resources in workplaces. There are rising levels of stress-related illness and
early retirement in many of our countries as we discussed in Chapter 2. Those who are
able to make time for leisure often find that this enhances their performance at work, as
illustrated by the Norwegian government official discussed above. Similarly, friendships,
whether at work or beyond, like other aspects of personal life may be viewed as competing with time at work, but others take a more synergistic and long-term perspective and
see the decline in friendships or other relationships as unsustainable. It can put pressure
on people at the psychological and emotional levels, which may ultimately affect performance at work as well as individual well-being.

> What is making me feel scared is I am a relationship person and I really feel pained
> at the kind of quality of relationships which is happening to be lost, especially in the
> organisations, it's very superficial, and that puts pressure on people at the psycholo-
> gical level, the emotional level, and I am seeing that to be in the long term will affect
> productivity because if you don't have a sense of belonging and don't belong to where
> you go to work you just cannot sustain that kind of an environment, you just cannot.
> At the end of the day your heart should be happy and you should have that sense of
> belonging. (Indian man, manager)

We argue that fostering well-being, care and connectedness across multiple aspects of
life, including paid work, is crucial for long-term sustainability.

Other sustainability issues include falling birth rates and the quality of care people are
able to give and receive as discussed in Chapter 3. In many countries, particularly those
with low levels of social provisions for carers, a strategy for managing both heavy work
demands and family and other commitments is to limit family size or not to have children
(see Transition Research Report #1, 2003). The low birth rate, in turn, can also exacerbate care of the elderly issues as there are fewer younger people to care for ageing populations. For example, in Japan we hear:

> It's not that women don't want children. It's just in reality; it is very hard and expen-
> sive to combine work and child care. Work and family are not compatible. (Japanese
> man, government advisor)

> Today's young people are sandwiched between the wish to have children and also they realise that the social security system, the pensions, won't endure. So if they can not have that money, they have to save for their old age and Japan has the highest longevity in the world so you have to be really wealthy and how they cut their expenses is not having children. (Japanese woman, NGO)

As discussed in Chapter 2, fertility rates are a particular concern in Japan, where government and business are concerned about future sustainability of the economy because of falling numbers of workers and consumers. Concerns about the future of the economy because of declining birth rates are also increasingly felt in other countries. This is prompting many policy initiatives to support childcare. Yet there is also some debate about the desirability of promoting this purely on the basis of seeing children as future citizen-workers, to bolster the economy, rather than focusing on the care of children and their well-being as important activities in their own right (Lister, 2004). 'Children are not seen as a social good and family care is not valued as an occupation, which means people continue to work hard in paid employment . . . we are teaching our kids to have the same pattern of over work that we have' (American country meeting).

The growing invasiveness of paid work can have negative impacts on families and care relationships in 'developing' countries too. A United Nations (1999) report finds that exportation of western patterns of work that take little account of other responsibilities or needs in life are resulting in crises of child, elder and disability care with critical social consequences globally. Families living in poverty across the world often have to contend with employers who do not take account of family needs and this can undermine vaccination or other health care programmes, for example, as taking time off work to take children to clinics results in loss of pay (Heymann et al., 2004). Research in a range of developing countries and among the poor in the USA also demonstrates how employers can impose working conditions that can force parents to leave children home alone or in the charge of older children who are taken out of school (www.globalworkingfamilies.org). Often parents, usually mothers, face stark choices between caring for and providing economically for families. In some contexts, children may have to be carers too. For example: 'My sense is that people will just have to give up work if they have to care for someone or rely on extended family members . . . sometimes in the very poorer communities, the burden might fall on children to be carers. They will be taken out of school' (South African man, social worker).

The sustainability of communities is also threatened by lack of time for community participation and also by the movement of jobs in the global economy, as we mentioned in Chapter 4. There is much consensus that community is important for human well-being and sustainability and likely to become more rather than less so. For example, a South African man working with people infected with HIV/AIDS recognises the need for workplaces and families to change to accommodate the caring issues involved. He also believes, however, that communities now hold the key to future supports for those affected by the virus.

> We need to rethink family and the notion of the extended family, for example. We call it the over extended family. It's too simple to say the extended family will take care of people because firstly it doesn't exist anymore with urbanisation and migration – one is cut off from extended families, or the extended family is too stretched and in fact many general household incomes have become lower and lower – if more children come to the family, then they are just depleting the resources. We do need to think about maybe communities coming together to offer care, to set up little homes, rethinking families is important. (South African, AIDS worker)

In this chapter we have argued that:

- current ways of harmonising work with personal life in which paid work is so dominant, affects care and connectedness in families, communities and friendships
- this can result in loneliness and other forms of disconnection
- all this has critical consequences for equity, well-being and sustainability.

Thus, it is important to reflect on the kind of societies we want, including how we care for and care about people with different needs, at various phases of the life course. To conclude, we return to our five Cs and argue that in the context of competitive global *capitalism* and growing *consumerism* where *commitment* is defined much more in terms of time in paid work than time in families or communities, paid work is increasingly undermining the time, energy and value given to *care* and *connectedness*, sometimes with crucial consequences. This raises deeper questions about how to move forward by enabling people to have more time and energy for enriched life experiences across multiple parts of life. It also raises deeper questions about what is valued by people and societies more generally.

The next chapter explores critical connections and interactions between harmonising paid work with other parts of life and relationships between men and women.

CHAPTER 6

Reciprocal Relationships between Men and Women: A Critical Issue

In all seven countries the invasiveness of paid work and the increasing sense of identity derived from it, have reduced the time for – and sometimes the value attached to – care and connectedness in families, communities and other domains of life. Given the consequences for equity, well-being and sustainability, we argue that workplaces and other institutions need to change. Yet another critical and connected part of the picture is that men and women's roles and relationships and their particular attachments to work and family spheres need to evolve further in reciprocal and dynamic ways. This is not easy. The separation of paid work and family life, one associated with men and the other with women, has perpetuated particular assumptions about 'ideal' workers as well as 'ideal' carers. Women often face – and are expected to face – psychological, emotional and practical pulls and demands from the domestic sphere and men from paid work. So assumptions about what it means to be a 'man' or a 'woman' are deeply ingrained in individuals' identities and wider societal expectations about what these identities should be. These assumptions are not static. Individuals and societies are at different stages of evolution in terms of men and women's identities and relationships. In this chapter we highlight the need for various kinds of reciprocal changes between men and women in the context of harmonising paid work with family and personal life. We then explore barriers and resistances to these varying changes at multiple levels, including the very personal individual level and the ways this interacts with barriers in families and workplaces in different societies.

BRINGING MEN INTO THE PICTURE

Many women's roles have changed dramatically in all the countries in our study over the past half century, as discussed in Chapter 2. There is also some change in men's behaviour in all the countries, although there are variations in the way that this is discussed, for example in terms of men 'helping' women or as doing a more equal share of family work. This reflects stages of evolution in men and women's identities and relationships.

> Men are definitely more involved in children. When I was young you never saw a man in the playground or pushing a carriage or anything. Now you see it all the time. (American woman, academic)

> Men are changing and they have changed significantly . . . in my own family, I don't think my father would ever have been able to make a cup of tea for himself . . . but

> today, seeing a daughter who goes out to work, I notice he is doing more . . . and fathers are more aware that they have a role to play with children . . . men want to spend more time with their families. (Indian woman, executive)

> I have always taken the view that you have to include men. And I am seeing some change in their behaviour. They are helping more in the home. (Japanese woman, government advisor)

> Men are experiencing a loss of time with their families and there is a ground swell of feeling and concern about this. (South African woman, academic)

However, the degree and level of change amongst men has been much slower than change amongst women, everywhere.[1] One factor holding back change is prevailing assumptions about 'ideal' carers – a role and identity associated with women. This not only underpins the tendency for employed women to retain the major responsibility for childcare or other care, but can also exclude men from becoming more involved in parenting or other forms of caring activities. For example, researchers have long examined the effect of maternal employment on children, but rarely consider the impact of fathers' employment on their children,[2] even though there is recent evidence that paternal care involvement – and shared care by mothers and fathers – can be beneficial for child development and well-being (Burgess & Russell, 2003).[3] If men are often excluded from discussions about parenting and other forms of caring roles and, if they perceive discussions about harmonising or combining various parts of life as focused solely on combining paid work and care responsibilities, they may see this as a woman's issue, not relevant to them.[4] They can then absent themselves from discussions. 'You go along to these work–life balance events and how many men do you see there? Often I'm the only one' (British man, small business owner).

Yet men are as central to these challenges and debates as women.

> Women have run God knows how many laps of the equality race . . . if men aren't engaged it will just go round and round in circles. (British man, journalist)

> As long as we talk in terms of women and childcare it remains a woman's issue. So I firmly believe that this is something we have to broaden to include men. And this is beginning to change. (British woman, trade union)

---

[1] For example, Hobson and Morgan (2002, p. 3) note that 'time budget studies show that, while men's involvement in unpaid care work has increased slightly in some countries, it is a drop in the bucket in relation to the loss in women's full-time care work', which they note is often characterised as a care deficit in the context of child, elder and disability care.

[2] Gornick and Meyers (2003, pp. 242–245; 249–255) synthesize evidence about the effects of maternal employment on child well-being, finding that children whose mothers are employed during the first year may fare worse than children whose mothers are not employed and that for children in formal childcare, the quality of provision matters greatly. However, while they are also interested in assessing policy provisions on gender equity, they highlight that little research has focused on the impacts of paternal involvement on child well-being.

[3] See Flouri (2005), who offers a comprehensive analysis of fathering and child outcomes and concludes that the impact of fathering depends on what is meant by 'good' fathering, what child outcomes are considered and what groups of parents and children are looked at. See also O'Brien (2005), writing in a UK context, who explores motivations for and impacts of paternal involvement in child care; discusses the contentious notions of what care and shared care may imply; and suggests a number of potential policy developments and challenges.

[4] In terms of male exclusion from discussions about their caring roles and activities in the context of harmonising paid work with other parts of life, illuminating insights are offered by Hawkins and Dollahite (1997), who discuss the continued emphasis on the inadequacy and resistance of fathers' involvement in care roles without paying sufficient emphasis to the constraints that exist. They thus discuss the need to move beyond these deficit perspectives by exploring the attachment, desires and skills that men can bring to childcare. See also Burgess and Russell (2003), who discuss deficit perspectives, and negative discourses, about the ways in which assumptions about fathers' 'non-interest' or competency can be implied across a range of government and workplace policies and discourses. This can encourage researchers, practitioners, policy makers and family members (including men themselves) to form negative opinions concerning fathers' motives and behaviour in the context of care involvement.

> Women tend to immediately take up on care when children are born. Both parents
> should work part-time and divide child care tasks as well . . . women should lay back
> some more, so men are forced to make the next move. (female participant, The
> Netherlands country meeting)

The need to bring men into debates about strategies for harmonising paid work with
other parts of life is recognised in some countries more than others (see Chapter 2). For
example, in Norway government policies and initiatives such as the 'daddy month' of
parental leave are designed specifically to encourage change in men's roles, at least as
fathers, and to enable some reciprocal change in women. 'The best way to somehow
improve equality is where men do more family and women can also do more of what they
would like to do . . . you have to move in both directions. I think that is where we are
really ahead in Norway' (Norway, woman manager).

The nature and extent of change amongst men in the different countries and the ways
in which this is discussed – for example as 'helping' women or as deeper reciprocal change
– are influenced by historical and evolutionary contexts.[5] This in turn influences the possibilities of further reciprocal changes in women's roles and relationships.

THE NEED FOR RECIPROCAL CHANGE IN MEN

As women are more involved in paid work, there is a need for men to change their behaviour and orientation towards family and paid work. Without such reciprocal change, 'ideal'
worker and 'ideal' carer assumptions continue. Many women will continue to be penalised
in workplaces and it will remain difficult for men to be more involved in family life and
other non-paid activities. This reciprocity of change is an ongoing and dynamic process,
again influenced by historical and evolutionary contexts. If men do change, women are
enabled or required to change further, for example, by relinquishing their roles as main
carers and this can feel difficult.[6] Yet without these ongoing reciprocal changes, the evolution of men and women's roles and relationships with each other and the ways in which
they can harmonise paid work with family and personal lives will remain stuck.

There is a need to emphasise the reciprocal opportunities men and women can gain from
evolving roles and relationships. Reciprocal change can offer women more opportunities
for inclusion and advancement in paid work and it can bring men greater opportunities for
involvement in family and other non-paid parts of life.

---

[5] To use the example of fathering again, Hobson (2002) includes chapters on the different ways in which fathers are viewed and
constructed within particular policy contexts in a range of countries. For example, in a chapter on the Dutch situation, by
Trudie Knijn and Peter Selten (2002), a new emphasis has been placed on fathers and their caring role including media campaigns, joint custody laws and innovative policies to encourage and enable both mothers and fathers to reconcile paid work
with family life. However, the authors also note labour market demands and expectations can result in many constraints for
fathers to change their behaviour. In contrast, in a chapter on the UK context, Jane Lewis (2002) argues that in comparison to
Scandinavian countries in which there is more emphasis on fathers' caring roles, the debate in the UK puts more emphasis on
fathers' cash providing roles particularly in relation to absent fathers and their 'flight from commitment'. She notes that the
importance of the caring role of fathers has only recently begun to receive more policy attention. Since the time of writing,
increasing emphasis – or at least lip-service – is placed on father's caring roles in the context of policy developments we document in Chapter 2, including growing attention to actively enabling fathers to care (see Stanley, 2005). So here we see evidence of some evolution.

[6] Allen and Hawkins (1999) find evidence of maternal gatekeeping in historical and contemporary contexts by synthesizing literature and conducting a contemporary analysis of American data on a number of factors. Although they discuss limitations
with their analysis, they find that significant factors including the extent to which women redo household jobs done by men,
the feeling that women like to be in charge of the domestic arena, and a belief that others make judgements about how good
a wife/mother they are on the basis of how well cared for their homes and children.

> 'I almost visualise it now as men and women are sitting across the table from each other each has a gift for the other, neither, neither is quite prepared to hand over the gift because they aren't sure if they're going to get the other one back, and in many cases, we might not know what we're going to get from it' (British man, researcher).

Yet, simply to demand that men change misses many of the particular complexities, uncertainties and resistances that are evident across all the countries in our study at their different stages in this dynamic evolutionary process. These uncertainties and resistances are manifested in different ways. Central tensions include: whether men actually want to change; whether men will be enabled to make reciprocal changes at workplaces and other levels; and whether women will accept men entering domestic and care realms that have been so closely associated with female identity.

BARRIERS TO RECIPROCAL CHANGE AMONG MEN AND WOMEN

Many of the apparent barriers to reciprocal change in men and women's identities and relationships can be explained in terms of experiences of power and competition. The role of power in holding back change is discussed from a number of different perspectives. Pay differences between men and women are one example that contributes to assumptions that it is more 'rational' for men to concentrate on paid work and women on family care. Another example comes from men and women's potential uneasiness about making fundamental changes to ways in which they combine different aspects of life – because of the status and power paid work can offer men or the power that involvement in family life can offer women.

> What's the incentive for men to change? That's the kind of big question that doesn't have a satisfactory answer . . . to do so, would mean losing power, and this is seen as a crap deal. (British man, researcher)

> There is always money and power involved. Trying to find equitable solutions means you have the problems of empowering women, which is often seen as disempowering for men . . . sometimes this can lead to conflict or even violence. (South African woman, trade union)

> Women use the children as a power institution. They say the child is more connected to them . . . they build a kind of fortress around the child and the men often stays scratching on the outside, wanting to come in. The woman only opens the door when it suits her and that is unfair on the men. (Norwegian woman, scientist)

Men and women may fear giving up things that are important to them without receiving anything in return. Reciprocal change requires moving away from competition between men and women towards providing both with a wider range of opportunities for equitable relationships. Yet people in the seven different countries, in the meetings and individual interviews, discuss competition that often exists between men and women, which can discourage reciprocal change. 'Women have been so assertive about the need for them to be in high positions . . . and doing that makes men afraid, because it becomes competitive. We have to work around this and talk with men about how we can work better together instead of competing and respect the differences' (Norway, government official).

These barriers contribute to resistances to change.

RESISTANCES TO CHANGE

Resistance to change in men and women's roles and relationships occurs at the level of individual identities, as well as within families, in workplaces and wider societies. When people try to change the ways in which they behave or think, this can challenge personal identity and beliefs about what it means to be a 'man' or a 'woman'.[7] There can also be interpersonal tensions amongst couples trying to adapt to change, intergenerational conflicts of expectations, and tensions arising from persisting workplace cultures and practices, government policy and wider societal assumptions. Conflicts and tensions in relation to male and female roles and relationships in the context of harmonising work with other parts of life are experienced differently by men and women within and across the different countries in our study. For example, in Norway, where there is much consensus and support for men to change, discussions amongst our participants highlight the difficulties women can feel in further reciprocal change about sharing care with men.

> 'We are talking about a transition not just for men, but for many women. A lot of women are unprepared in practice to take the full implications of it, which means actually giving up some control over how things are done in the home and relationships with children. This is a division that has to be reworked . . .' (Norwegian woman, IT consultant).

In the UK, where there has been less support for men to change, current discussions often focus on ways to get men more involved in family life. However, there is also growing recognition of the need for reciprocal change in women.

> 'A man wanting to be more involved in children and the home is a huge challenge for women, because they have to give up control of these issues and accept that men won't do things in the same way . . . this is an enormous challenge for women who are steeped in a culture of their own superiority in this area' (British man, researcher).

However, in South Africa, where race equity has dominated much recent discussion, we hear equity between men and women remains much more silenced and marginalised.

> 'We see a total unawareness and trivialisation of gender as an issue in South Africa, and a lack of understanding and skill to identify and challenge gender issues . . . race has been much more of an issue' (South African woman, human resource manager).

These differences relate to particular historical legacies, ideologies and debates.

Individual Identities

Assumptions about what it means to be male or female are internalised from a very early age. Notions of masculinity and femininity become ingrained in the identities of boys and girls from the moment they are born. The first question asked when a child is born is usually whether it is a boy or a girl and this affects the ways in which people relate to and treat the child. The assumptions made are then reinforced but sometimes challenged through experiences and interactions across the life course. The feminist movement has

---

[7] See West and Zimmerman (1987), who argue that gender identity and behaviour is not only imposed on individuals through structured forms of socialization but that individuals actively participate in the construction of their gender identity and behaviour. Gender identity is then seen as being actively worked out, revised, and sustained by individuals immersed in socially and historically constructed webs of power relations (see Sabo & Gordon, 1995). Gender, then, may be seen as 'something that one does, and does repeatedly in interaction with others' (West & Zimmerman, 1987, p. 140). See also Woodward, 2000.

created clear challenges to 'traditional' assumptions about male and female roles and identities, as have practical pressures women have faced in combining work with family life (see de Beauvoir, 1953; Friedan, 1963; Greer, 1971; Oakley, 1974). More recently, discussions of the ways in which notions of masculinity also limit opportunities and well-being for men have emerged in certain contexts (see Burgess & Russell, 2003; Connell, 1987). Yet assumptions about what it means to be a man or a woman are remarkably resistant to change. Change is not just a question of unlearning old patterns. Behaving in ways that go against deeply held assumptions about 'appropriate' male and female behaviour can be uncomfortable, threatening and painful. For example, many men struggle to adapt their identities to evolving roles and expectations and this is also related to the reactions of others around them.

> Men seem to be struggling with their identity and they have mental blocks over how they see it as possible to feel like a man. Their identity remains very closely identified to paid work . . . (Japanese woman, manager)

> It's like society does not recognise it, so I mean, for example, by any chance if we had the kind of money we wanted and he did choose to stay at home, my God, everyone would say 'Oh my God, what is he trying to do. I mean, he's such a loser', you know. (Indian woman, counsellor)

Similarly, behaving in ways that go against deeply held assumptions about 'appropriate' behaviour for women can also feel uncomfortable or threatening.

> I think women have been socialised over the generations to the nurturing role of the family. No matter how achievement orientated the woman is, she still feels obligations to children, to the family, to the partner. I think that's very powerful. Intellectually, women might think no, no, no, no. But deep-down, I think this motivates her. (British man, psychologist)

Interestingly these quotes above are either women talking about men's experiences or men talking about women's. They may well relate to stereotypes. However, these anxieties can engender fear and guilt and these feelings can make it difficult for men and women to talk about their own dilemmas. Often they become silenced and taboo.[8]

> I think it takes women to help acknowledge men's abilities as fathers and as carers. But the response from women to this is like walking into a minefield . . . men involved in thinking about these issues are so aware of equality and political correctness, that it can hold them back or inhibit them from saying things they think. A lot of things are thought but not said. (British man, journalist)

> I'm an active feminist, and I know it is important to share responsibilities with men in the home . . . but, if I'm being, well, really honest, it's not easy . . . I guess I feel it's my body, I'm the one who had children, I feel a sense of ownership in a way . . . I also find it difficult to fully trust him when he is looking after the kids . . . I worry that he is doing other things and not giving them enough attention . . . there are so many contradictions . . . those have been really big tensions throughout my life, but its

---

[8] Gender can often be a taboo issue in itself, which was raised implicitly or explicitly in all the countries in our study. To talk about gender relationships raises issues of identity which people find hard to do, and this can be linked back to fear. To operate within existing gender identities and frameworks can provide meaning and rationality to people which, according to MacInnes (1998), became increasingly important during the enlightenment period when so many other meaning systems were challenged. To challenge gender roles, identities and relationships can disrupt people's internal meaning systems as it can unearth many deep-rooted – but socially constructed – personal assumptions about who people are and why they behave as they do. These fears prevent open and honest dialogue between women and men, which impede changes within men and women's identities and relationships between them. For gender equity to be a reality it needs discussing at all levels of society. But whilst it remains taboo and seen as difficult to raise, inequities will persist. This will affect the extent to which people can achieve equitable, sustainable and satisfying harmonisation of paid work and personal life.

hard to be honest about this when you are fighting for change. (British woman, trade unionist)

We also hear of another fear: that moving too far away from stereotypical male or female behaviour may make them less sexually attractive, although this was not a widely articulated view.

> I think a man feels it's not his attractiveness that attracts a woman but how successful he is ... So if that's the case, if a man let's go of being achievement driven, will he lose the woman? ... when I asked a women how she copes with a less successful man, I got the feeling that she had a lot of trouble ... she said 'you know there is something in this, it's not just he's threatened by me, but I wonder sometimes whether, whether I need somebody as successful as me' ... So I just wonder if men are reluctant to let go [of their primary association with paid work] because they think they won't be as attractive to women unless they are successful in whatever the hell they are doing. (British man, senior manager, public sector)

Couple and Family Relationships

These individual identity issues can create tensions in interpersonal relationships in couples and families. In heterosexual couple relationships, resistance to change tends to reflect the phase of evolution of men and women's roles and relationships in the wider society, although these can be experienced in different ways. In more 'traditional' contexts, for example, both men and women can be resistant to changes in domestic roles, and this can make it difficult for women to move beyond social expectations about 'appropriate' roles. 'My husband says "why should I deprive you of doing what you are best at?" And on making a bed, he would say, "no, I am airing it". And you end up doing it because you don't want an untidy bedroom ... people would see it when they come to the house' (South African woman, NGO worker).

This is not limited to 'traditional' contexts, however. Powerful social expectations can perpetuate 'traditional' male and female identities, roles and relationships across more 'developed' societies. 'If I complain about how dirty the house is, he just says he doesn't mind, so I end up cleaning it. I know it shouldn't be this way, but it is very hard to let go. I worry if the house is dirty and what people will think ...' (Dutch woman, researcher).

It is interesting that evidence suggests that the division of paid and unpaid work is more fluid amongst same-sex couples. Gillian Dunne, for example, finds that lesbian couples are able to transcend assumptions about who will be the main earner and who will do the unpaid work. She finds lesbian couples can be less constrained than opposite-sex couples in developing innovative patterns of sharing roles and responsibilities (Dunne, 2000).

Because of individual identity issues, discussed above, the relationships of some opposite-sex couples can also be threatened if women are seen to be too successful in the workplace. For example, we hear in India that some women who are given promotions at work may keep this from their husband until he has caught up in terms of workplace development. Similar stories were told by some women in the Dutch country meeting.

Nevertheless, some opposite-sex couples are also able to transcend 'traditional' role expectations. However, progress is rarely straightforward and partners face new identity issues along the way. To illustrate, we return to two of the characters who we introduced in our Dutch opening story in the Prologue, Johan and Anna's friends: Tanja and Hans.

Despite commitment to a life in line with their egalitarian beliefs, with both of them working part-time and sharing the care at home, Tanja was finding it a real struggle. It wasn't so much her pressures at work, but more from trying to deal with the fact that Hans seemed better with their children than she was. She couldn't fault him. The way they organised their lives had been something they had long discussed and had worked hard to achieve. When they married both changed their family names as a symbol of their egalitarian beliefs; they bottle-fed both their children so they could both form strong – and equal – nurturing bonds with them; and they had both reduced their hours at work. But it wasn't as easy as she thought it would be. She couldn't shake the feeling that it didn't feel quite right. She resented the ways the children responded to Hans, and she was jealous of some of her women friends who seemed to be closer to their children. She felt unneeded – Hans could do everything – conned and a little betrayed.

As men become more involved with and attached to their children, challenging 'ideal' worker and women as carer assumptions, new conflicts can emerge. Change always creates tensions, which is evident in progressive families particularly when relationships go wrong and it is no longer automatically the mother who has exclusive or privileged access to the children.

> There is a conflict between men and women when men are more caring for the home and their children. There is often more fighting and there can be more divorce. The fighting increases because men are more attached to the children and in divorces their role is no longer simply to provide income, there are more feelings involved. (Norwegian woman, manager)

In other contexts, intergenerational conflicts can arise if younger men and women attempt to have more equitable relationships with each other, particularly if they live in joint families. In India, for example, one couple we spoke with, who lived with the husband's parents, tried to challenge the father's expectations about the role and responsibilities of his daughter-in-law. The father expected his daughter-in-law to stop or reduce her participation in paid work so as to concentrate on having children and cook for the family. The younger couple wanted to defend their own values and decisions but they were reluctant to create tensions at home. As the younger husband told us:

> There was a lot of tension in my mind. On the one hand I felt very strongly about this ... and on the other hand I didn't want to damage permanently my relationship with my father ... throughout our childhood he [my father] was extremely modern in his outlook and then I got married and we stayed with my parents for the first ... six or seven months ... all of a sudden, he became a traditional father-in-law and now he wanted Ajara to start behaving like a traditional daughter-in-law in the house and we kind of thought it was a new, new daughter-in-law syndrome ... initially I let it go ... he would say ... I want [to eat] what Ajara has made. So initially my mother would try and cover up because my father has a vicious temper ... and then, one fine day I just lost it, I said no I'm sorry [she] has not made anything and she's not going to until you and I also make something. (Indian man, business consultant)

Intergenerational conflicts about equity between men and women are not unique to societies in which joint family living arrangements are common. In Norway, for example, one leading female scientist, talked about how her mother and other women of that generation would berate her for working too hard and not spending enough time with the children. Yet nobody criticised her husband in this way.

Resistance in Workplaces and Other Institutions

Just as changes in women's behaviours and values requires reciprocal change in men, so changes within families require changes in workplaces. Many workplaces acknowledge the importance of adapting to the changing needs of women, although this is often superficial, for example involving so called 'family-friendly' or 'work–life' policies. However, despite attention to work and family issues, workplaces have been slow to fully recognise the need to adapt organisational norms, structures and cultures to reflect or enable changing relationships between men and women (see, for example, Bailyn, 1993; Lewis, 1997; Lewis, S., 2001; Rapoport et al., 2002). In South Africa, despite crises in care due to the HIV/AIDS epidemic, we were told that: 'It is assumed men are not involved with caring and they often get left out when it comes to opportunities to change their working practices' (attendee, South African country meeting).

The same neglect of men's family needs is true in workplaces in many other contexts. Consequently, many men remain unable or reluctant to make significant changes in paid work and other parts of their life, and many women continue to be marginalised in the workplace (Butler & Skattebo, 2004; Lewis, 1997; Smithson, 2005). In all seven countries, some men and women are openly discussing interpersonal and workplace tensions, conflicts and practical difficulties they face in harmonising the multiple parts of their lives. Yet many men are reluctant to raise these issues with their bosses or colleagues, because they feel it may be interpreted as a lack of commitment in the context of current assumptions about 'ideal' workers. Few men, in any of the countries in our study, are demanding change in the workplace to match changes in the home. When they do so, they can be penalised even in progressive contexts, as we saw in Chapter 4 in the story of Per, one of our Norwegian characters.

In many contexts women are still struggling overtly to be accepted by men in the workplace and this is particularly so in India and Japan. For example, in Japan, senior women are often asked to make the tea by male colleagues and in recruitment processes, they can be asked about their virginity and other personal factors.[9] In India, it is acceptable for men to admit to their uneasiness about accepting women in senior positions. For example, at the Indian country meeting participants talked about courses that had been run recently in Bangalore entitled 'How to Deal with your Woman Manager'. This would be politically incorrect in contexts where equal rights legislation and a plethora of 'work–family' initiatives contribute to a myth of 'post-feminism' and assumptions that these tensions no longer exist.[10] In these contexts, people often view difficulties in relationships between men and women in the workplace and beyond as isolated or individual problems.

There are also resistances to reciprocal changes in men and women's relationships and identities at government levels. Governments vary in responses to and initiatives on harmonising paid work with other parts of life, but most are resistant to intervening in the 'private' world of men–women relationships, seeking instead quick fixes for dealing with complex dilemmas. In practice, many policies do little to enable men and women to work through many tensions and conflicts that arise between them. This can perpetuate men's

---

[9] See Blau, Ferber and Winkler (2002). While this study focuses on the USA, the authors include a particularly interesting and useful chapter setting these issues in an international context, in which they document experiences in a range of countries, including Japan.

[10] Coppock, Haydon and Richter (1995) discuss the ways in which equal opportunities legislation, which is unsubstantiated by enabling factors such as funded childcare or leaves or active strategies to include men in care roles, can mean women internalize failings to succeed in paid work as their own fault rather than seeing structural or cultural constraints.

lesser involvement in unpaid work and the trade-offs women feel compelled to make in relation to employment and caring responsibilities.[11]

Even when individuals, couples, workplaces and governments are more open to change, other institutions can often lag behind. For example, legal systems tend to favour mothers in child custody cases in divorce rather than supporting joint custody arrangements, although our Norwegian participants believe that this is being challenged to some extent in Norway. Even in Europe, where there has been considerable change in family relationships, the European Court of Justice still upholds assumptions of the 'ideal' parent as a mother and can overturn and undermine progress that has been made in individual member states.[12]

THE GLOBAL CONTEXT

Challenges faced in the context of reciprocal change between men and women are exacerbated in all seven countries by prevailing models of global competitive capitalism and growing consumerism. Transformations in and speeding up of paid work and increasing consumer wants or desires in the global economy exacerbate assumptions about 'ideal' workers in many different contexts. Workplace demands and expectations make it even more difficult for women and men to work through conflicts and tensions about their identities and the ways this relates with current patterns of harmonising paid work with other parts of life.

> Women's aspirations and wanting to work coincided at a time when economic trends of work intensification really began to let rip. And you got this awful crunch where our aspirations went smack up against an accelerating economic trend. (British woman, journalist)

> I have friends in the Oslo area . . . they have big jobs, big salaries, everything in order but they are stressed and their life is not so good. They want equality in the family but they can't keep it up. There are so many pressures at work . . . downsizing to keep up with world competition, you know . . . their wives decide to stop working for a while to care for the children and this is a good idea . . . but it should also be the husband of course. (Norwegian man, entrepreneur)

Many people in the seven countries feel that dilemmas about combining paid work with care responsibilities seem to have increased as the demands of paid work become ever more acute. This can reduce perceived opportunities for men and women to combine paid work with family life in diverse ways. 'There are two trends in response to the current situation of long hours. The first is a return to traditional gender roles in families, and the

---

[11] Daly and Rake (2003, p. 173) discuss EU inspired work–family reconciliation policies and note that 'it is significant that these are framed as "family-friendly" rather than as gender equality measures. They do not in practice do much to increase men's involvement in unpaid work or to significantly ameliorate the trade-offs involved for women'. See also Lister (2003, Chapter 7) and Lewis, J. (2001), who argues that no welfare state has managed to fully value the unpaid work in families, which is primarily performed by women. We would extend this observation to argue that no society more generally, including those without a 'welfare state', has managed to value or seek adequate strategies to harmonise or share unpaid work done in families with employment in gender equitable ways. See also Knijn (2000), for example, who argues that welfare state cutbacks or pressures can increase the expectation that combining paid work with other parts of life requires individual strategies. Knijn notes that welfare retrenchments place more pressures on families to provide care without sufficient supports for families to do this.

[12] See McGlynn (2001), who explores the legacy of maternal attachment theories and the influence of psychologists such as John Bowlby and the ways in which judges in the European Court of Justice have often displayed support for these notions through rulings that counter certain country attempts for more fluid and equitable roles for men and women.

other is having no children. Neither is life affirming . . . it is not that people are actively choosing these options, they just don't have other options . . . especially for the low paid' (American man, professor).

Trends, such as the intensification and extension of work, can jeopardise the fragile progress that has been made in evolving relationships between men and women and in related workplace changes. This in turn can further restrict perceived opportunities to downshift or collaborate creatively with others in finding new ways to work that take greater account of diverse personal lives.

CONSEQUENCES FOR EQUITY, WELL-BEING AND SUSTAINABILITY

All these barriers and resistances, together with trends in current forms of global competitive capitalism, perpetuate inequities between men and women, at the workplace level, in families and in other social institutions as we discussed in Chapters 4 and 5.

The progress made in workplaces to accommodate changes in men–women relationships and identities is uneven, even in Norway, and indeed recent trends such as the intensification of work and other ramifications of global competitiveness have created new pressures (Brandth & Kvande, 2001; 2002). In these environments men and women can feel enormous pressures to 'have and do it all', which impacts on well-being. One consequence is that women in senior positions in paid work in some countries are dropping out and rejecting the 'superwoman' image (Marshall, 1995).

> 'It's taken for granted that girls growing up should get an education and get a job, many of their mothers did it. Perhaps then, the goal was self realisation. But now . . . I talk to a lot of women who think they work too much and they think it is too much pressure on the family' (British woman, manager).

In Norway, where men–women relationships have made much progress, we hear men too talk about the pressures they feel to be 'super-beings'.

> 'Male friends say now it is a hell of a rat race; they have to have a good career, be nice lovers, nice fathers, nice friends, nice intellectual talking partners and they say the pressure is coming at them from more fields' (Norwegian woman, scientist).

Men are also experiencing these pressures in other contexts, at different evolutionary points. For example in India:

> Some men are in transition with working wives. Men don't have the physical work of cooking or looking after children but they are having a psychological transition . . . they are feeling a role erosion away from the main breadwinner and the importance they got earlier. Their own sense of self worth and the way their own family perceives them has undergone a drastic change. (Indian woman, manager)

As long as men's identities are wholly tied up with success in paid work, which is increasingly invasive and demanding, it will be difficult for men to change. Not only does this hold back reciprocal change between men and women but as one participant points out, it can have serious consequences for health and well-being.

> Men have to change. Maybe they are worried about how women will proceed if they let all the nurturing, feminine side of themselves come out. I think they are worried about that. Otherwise with all the pressures at work, the rise of heart disease in men,

their higher mortality and morbidity rates, why, when stress is bumping them off, do they not want to change? You'd think they'd be pleased to have this opportunity and shift down in a sense. But they're not. Something is stopping them. (British man, manager)

Implications for well-being and happiness were recognised in most of our country meetings. An Indian man reflected:

We couldn't, we couldn't [reverse the gender roles] because, because we've got used to a sort of a lifestyle where, where the kind of income that I am able to bring in helps us to maintain that lifestyle . . . , if I was to stop doing that . . . it wouldn't be enough to support the same sort of lifestyle, although I might actually be a little happier doing it. (Indian man, business consultant)

Much change in men–women relationships is held back by the need to reach or retain a certain lifestyle. However it is worth reflecting here on the recent work of Richard Layard (2003; 2005), a British economist. He argues that once incomes have risen above a certain level, so that basic needs are met, any further increases in earnings does not bring greater happiness. This amount is quite low. He calculates it stands at 15000 pounds sterling or equivalent. However, people get used to what they have and then face pressures to maintain these standards. People also have a desire to keep up with other people in material terms which, he suggests, might explain why happiness does not rise at the same rate as income levels past a certain point. He goes on to suggest that earning too much and the 'overwork' this can entail is a pollutant, which should be taxed, and that this would encourage a better 'work–life balance'.

Consumerism and meaning derived from paid work and possessions can thus slow down, or even reverse, evolutions of men and women's roles and relationships with each other. Current inequities and well-being problems, seen in all the countries in our study, pose questions about whether current forms of harmonising paid work with other parts of life can be sustained by individuals, families, workplaces and wider societies.

In this chapter we have argued that:

- Challenges about harmonising work with other parts of life are as central to men as to women, but men are often left out of discussions and initiatives for change.
- Any change in women's roles and identities requires reciprocal change in men, which may be different in different contexts at different points in time.
- Resistance to reciprocal change in men and women's roles and relationships occurs in various ways at the level of individual identities, as well as within families, and in workplaces.
- These resistances can be exacerbated by current forms of competitive global capitalism.
- Resistance to change has consequences for equity, well-being and sustainability for individuals, and in families, communities and workplaces.

As we concluded in the last two chapters, the way *commitment* is defined in current forms of *capitalism* along with growing *consumerism* undermines *care* and *connectedness*. This has crucial consequences for equity, well-being and sustainability. As well as a need for workplaces to change, these challenges are inherently related to reciprocal change between men and women. Thus, it is important to explore the interactions and reciprocity between men–women relationships and the harmonisation of work and other parts of life, at individual, systemic and societal levels at various stages of particular country evolutions.

Moving Forwards

CHAPTER 7

Visions and Strategies for Change

> It is time for a larger discussion about what combination of economic dynamism and
> social tranquillity we want for ourselves, our families, and our society; and about the
> public choices we need to make . . . Every society has the capacity – indeed the obli-
> gation – to make these choices. Markets are structured around them. Families and com-
> munities function according to them. Individuals balance their lives within them. It is
> through such decisions that a society defines itself. The choices will be made somehow.
> They cannot be avoided. The question is whether we make the most important of these
> choices together, in the open, or grapple with them alone and in the dark. (Reich, 2001,
> pp. 249–250)

If people cannot harmonise their lives in equitable and satisfying ways, individuals, families, communities and organisations will suffer. As business guru Charles Handy (1997,
p. 157) reminds us, 'capitalism as an idea includes social capital as well as economic capitalism. One without the other will not work for long'. As we have argued throughout this
book, to address equity, well-being and sustainability at one level, we have to think about
what changes are needed at other levels and this will require people to collaborate within
and across families, communities, workplaces and wider societies. For example, as discussed in Chapter 3, government initiatives to encourage fathers to be more involved in
family care require corresponding shifts in workplaces and families, including the questioning of assumptions about 'ideal' workers, 'ideal' carers and what it means to be a man
or a woman. Innovative approaches are needed that address multiple and interacting levels.
This is a huge challenge. It involves questioning many accepted wisdoms about how
society works and how people should behave.

> 'The work–life balance debate is actually on the edge of a much bigger problem. It all
> comes down to questioning and thinking about the ways in which capitalism has
> encouraged us to live our lives in particular ways' (British woman, NGO).

No wonder people feel powerless to make these changes alone. Without widespread reflection and collaboration, people will continue to grapple with important choices 'alone and
in the dark'.

How might it be possible to harness the discontents about current ways of working and
living that we have begun to uncover in this study and which are also evident in many
emerging social movements campaigning on issues ranging from free and fair trade to
environmental sustainability? How can perceived constraints and crises become catalysts
for positive social change? We have discussed some evidence that potential crises are
beginning to bring about progressive change. In The Netherlands, for example, escalating
sickness rates have triggered government funded initiatives to encourage part-time work
and innovative change strategies in workplaces (see Lewis & Cooper, 2005, pp. 124–125).

In Japan, the dramatic decline in the birth rate has prompted government initiatives to support working parents, to produce media campaigns about father roles, and to give some attention to workplace cultures and practices. These are only small steps but may be catalysts for further progressive change. In the UK, the concern with persions arising from ageing populations and the potential need to alter work practices over a longer period of the life course could be another example of a major social force for change. How can various emerging social forces come together to form a wider will for progressive change? And how can this be translated into practical strategies to enable people to harmonise the many parts of their lives in equitable, satisfying and sustainable ways?

We tried to address some of these questions in collaboration with our participants. Yet we were struck by how difficult it was to think about the bigger picture in our country meetings and interviews. Hence, for the final part of our project, we brought together some of our international participants to feed back and reflect on some of our findings and to try to break through this impasse, with the help of scenario planners. Scenario planning draws lessons from possible futures. It encourages thinking about the future rather than predicting it. Scenario techniques do not act as crystal balls: social and economic change can occur in multiple and sometimes unexpected ways. However, thinking about a range of *potential* futures, informed by reflections on past and present experiences, can challenge rigid thinking about accepted wisdoms. We did not expect solutions to complex problems but hoped that the scenario planning process would help us all to envisage some alternative futures and progressive strategies for harmonising paid work with other parts of life.

The meeting took place over two days, which is a very short time to discuss such huge issues. Ironically, as a result of our own funding and time constraints – including the difficulty of bringing busy people together for long periods – we fell into the trap we have been warning against throughout this book. We sought quick fixes to these huge challenges. Although we came up with some seeds of promising ideas – which demonstrates that collaborative thinking is a necessary and important part of change processes – we recognise that this requires ongoing and wider collaboration. We were reminded of the importance of time and space to break down assumptions and barriers at multiple levels, and for the creative thinking required to seed wider progressive change.

POSSIBLE FUTURES

While, unsurprisingly, we did not come up with a quick fix at our international scenario meeting, we did develop a scenario pathway framework (see Rapoport, Lewis & Gambles, 2005), to help us to think about possible futures. We have continued to reflect on the collaborative thinking in the scenario meeting and we have built on some of the ideas to develop possible future scenarios for some of our characters discussed in this book.

In particular, the scenario meeting pointed to the need to extend options and reduce constraints in the ways that people can harmonise paid work and the rest of life. Very often men and women think they 'choose' particular strategies. Yet they may do so within current constraints such as: lack of childcare; family leaves that may be available to women rather than men *and* women; pay gaps between men and women; particular notions of 'ideal' workers and 'ideal' carers; and assumptions about men and women's 'appropriate' or 'natural' roles. Of course there will always be some constraints, such as financial needs or caring obligations. However, even these can often be thought about in different ways if assumptions about the distribution of resources and the distribution of care responsibilities are challenged. For example, if caring is regarded and supported as a valuable life-enhancing activity for men as well as women, people may have more freedom to harmonise their paid and unpaid work in innovative ways. If caring activities and associated skills also become valued in workplaces – and viewed as important and feasible for men and women – then current assumptions about 'ideal' workers and undervaluing of 'feminine' skills may be challenged and the ways in which work is done rethought. On the other hand, if caring continues to be regarded as something that women are better at, and part-time or flexible workers remain undervalued, both men and women's options for harmonising the many parts of life will continue to be constrained.

Things evolve. So how might our characters' situations change or evolve to provide more options for equitable, satisfying and sustainable ways of harmonising paid work and the rest of life?

Scenario One: More of the Same

Despite the pressures and challenges associated with current ways of harmonising paid work with other parts of life, many people see no alternative. So, they continue to experience the many parts of their lives in fragmented and constrained ways. It is not just individuals who are constrained in this way. Governments and businesses often feel powerless to resist pressures to compete in the global economy. This creates situations in which so many demands are made on workers – and workers can often make so many demands on themselves – that people lack time, energy or resources to contemplate making changes to the ways they combine the different parts of their lives. If people do reflect on possible changes, they often face what can seem like insurmountable barriers. Hence, we might simply see more of the same.

With more of the same, many women will continue to face trade-offs between having either to combine long hours in paid work with other responsibilities or to reduce their involvement in paid work, suffering financial or career consequences, or personal deprivation, as a result. In other words, women with caring responsibilities are likely to face constraints of time or money. Men will also find it difficult to reduce the time and commitment they give to paid work and to be more involved in family care and other non-paid activities. So equity and well-being problems for men and women will continue. As paid work continues to intrude into many people's lives, burn-out and exhaustion may also increase, and opportunities for connecting with friends, families and communities are likely to remain elusive. Inequities between groups of people more generally within and across societies will also persist. Despite hearing in South Africa, for example, that people feel it is unethical for long working hours among the employed to exist alongside high unemployment rates, some people will remain work-rich and time-poor while others will have too much time on their hands and not enough work. The needs of current dominant forms of capitalism will continue to dominate over other needs of individuals, families and communities and this trend is likely to continue spreading around the world. Individuals, families, communities and workplaces are likely to suffer. Problems of care deficits or falling birth rates will persist and concerns about social justice and quality of life will continue. There are nevertheless likely to be short-term pay-offs.

We can see some of the advantages and disadvantages of 'more of the same' by exploring potential futures in this scenario using the cases of Elizabeth in the USA and Ravi in India.

Shortly after we met Elizabeth, as discussed in our Prologue, she received devastating news. Her husband, Tom, has found someone else and tells her the marriage is over. Tom wants to move out immediately. The children will live with their mother but Tom will contribute to their maintenance. Despite these changed circumstances, Elizabeth decides that with Enrika's help, she will continue to work just as hard and continue to juggle this with family responsibilities. On the positive side, unlike many single mothers, she has the resources to participate fully in paid work, retaining her financial security and maintaining contact with other adults. However, both she and Tom see little of the children who are trying to cope with the trauma of their parents' break-up. Elizabeth also has little time to visit her mother. She continues to feel exhausted and fears that in the years to come she will regret the time she might have spent with her mother and children, or even socialising with friends. She knows she is making even more demands on Enrika and feels bad about this. Now, however, especially as she is struggling without Tom, she sees little alternative to her current arrangements.

In India, despite Ravi's exhaustion and concerns about not being able to see his sick mother, he too sees no alternative to his current situation. He strives for and eventually gains promotion. His wife, Naila, also continues to work hard at the school to try to make a difference to the lives and fortunes of her pupils. On the positive side, Ravi and Naila manage to climb their respective career ladders and enhance their material living standards for themselves and their children. He also sends money back to his mother in the village. Yet he knows his mother wants more of his time rather than his money. His employer later announces that the company will be moving on to find cheaper labour elsewhere. Although he has developed skills and accrued possessions, he finds himself out of a job. To make matters worse, his mother dies shortly afterwards. He is wracked with guilt and asks himself if it was all worth it. Now he has time on his hands he reflects on what is important in life. There was no time to do this when he was working at the call centre. He is concerned about his family's financial situation and both Naila and he find it difficult to accept Naila as the sole breadwinner. This causes tensions between them.

This scenario thus perpetuates current patterns – and problems – that many men and women experience in combining the many parts of life. Extreme workplace demands and constant busyness can prevent people from thinking about what is important in life. Particular notions about men and women's 'appropriate' roles can create obstacles to greater freedom for people to develop and feel comfortable with different scenarios. There is also little time for sustaining relationships, or for connecting with others through friendship, leisure or community involvement in this scenario. The sustainability of this scenario – for meeting individual, social and organisational needs – is deeply questionable.

Scenario Two: Reverting to 'Traditional' Roles

Some dual-earner couples find it too much to combine paid work and care responsibilities in equitable and satisfying ways and attempt to revert to male breadwinner and female carer family patterns. Some couples experience 'traditional' patterns positively. This kind of separation of roles is not possible for everyone: it is not possible for lone parents or many low-income families. Even for those who feel this is the best solution in the absence of other foreseeable options, it is often experienced as a compromise and can lead to mutual resentment. Men and women continue to be constrained by prevailing assumptions about appropriate roles. At the moment, social prescriptions about appropriate behaviours for men and women and male–female wage gaps constrain choices for men to be family carers and women to be main breadwinners. 'Traditional' patterns can have some negative consequences for individuals, families, organisations and wider society in current contexts. For example, if women who stay home with children are not able to easily reintegrate into the workforce later, and the 'ideal' worker is viewed as someone who does not take breaks from full-time employment, this can reduce women's career opportunities and leave women vulnerable to dependence and poverty. This can also have negative impacts on organisations and wider societies. In the case of divorce, for example, this scenario can increase the risk of female and child poverty.[1] If women are not able to use their skills – or skills developed in caring roles are not valued – human resources in organisations can be depleted which in turn could harm national economies.

We can see some of the advantages and disadvantages of 'reverting to traditional roles' by exploring potential futures in this scenario using the cases of Zhilah in South Africa and Claire in the UK.

Zhilah's daughter has died of HIV/AIDS and she is now caring for her young grandchildren. Meanwhile, she is trying to compensate for her absences from work due to family crises by working extra hard. She is exhausted. Yet part-time work is not accommodated for someone at her level. What can she do? Eventually, despite her fears about being dependent on her husband, she leaves her job. Without an income of her own, she returns to live with her husband. He agrees to work more shifts to compensate for her lost income to support the family. So she looks after the grandchildren while he brings in a wage. On the positive side, this solution enables her to spend time with her grandchildren, to care for other children in the community and feel she is making a useful contribution. Yet she feels that she has sacrificed her opportunities in paid employment. She misses contact with colleagues and her financial independence. The skills she has built up at her workplace are also wasted: an 'individual' example of a blow to the national economy. Although she feels this is an immediate solution for her family, she also feels they are vulnerable. What will happen if her husband's violence reappears?

Claire in the UK has been thinking a lot about what 'success' really means. The children are only young once. Is it worth sacrificing time with them as they grow up just so she can build up her career? These concerns may seem almost luxurious in comparison with Zhilah's situation. Yet they are troubling to her. Moreover, they reflect pervasive expectations about 'ideal' workers and 'ideal' carers, especially mothers.

Claire has long harboured thoughts about downshifting to a part-time job and finally decides to take the plunge. Her manager agrees to her request but believes it is not possible to work in a managerial role part-time. So she is moved to a project that does not involve supervising others: a virtual demotion. She sees it as a temporary arrangement but her manager makes it very clear that there is no guarantee she will be able to get her former position back when she wants it. On the positive side she now has more time with her children, she is less exhausted and even has time to see friends. She also saves on

---

[1] See Dewilde (2002), who explores the financial consequences of divorce in a number of western societies. At the same time however, if women continue to live with their husbands and rely on their wages for financial resources, intra-household redistribution can often occur in inequitable ways leaving some women experiencing hidden poverty (see, for example, Pahl, 1989, for a full discussion).

childcare costs so the money is not too different from before. However, she finds her work-load is still intense – she does much more than her allotted part-time hours. At the same time, the work is less interesting and satisfying. When she tries to discuss her frustrations with her husband he cannot get beyond the idea that this was her 'choice'. He tells her she is lucky to have this opportunity – a 'luxury' that men do not have. This creates tension between them.

While this scenario may provide some opportunities for couples to harmonise paid work with other parts of life, with one concentrating more on care responsibilities and the other on paid work – and it may offer opportunities to lone parents or low income families if financial supports are in place – there are also many problems. Without changes in work-places that enable Zhilah to work part-time or enable Claire to continue to make full use of her skills albeit in a part-time position for a short phase in her life, this scenario involves trade-offs and risks – usually for women, as in these two cases.[2] At the same time, without changes in both workplace and family contexts and interacting beliefs about men and women's appropriate roles, men have fewer opportunities to change the ways they work that may offer them time and energy for other parts of their lives. The inequities between men and women and stresses they face, discussed in earlier chapters, continue.

For some, separating roles is a satisfying experience of harmonisation. For others, this is experienced as fragmentation of work, family, and men and women's roles. Some feel they have the freedom and opportunity to choose this lifestyle. Many other choices, however, such as men staying at home, or men and women sharing paid work and care and enjoyment or leisure in more flexible and equitable ways, are constrained. They cannot even be visualised. The challenge is to envisage future scenarios in which a whole range of options is possible for both men and women.

Scenario Three: Innovative Strategies at Multiple Levels

More innovative scenarios would offer a range of possible options – and freedoms – for men and women to harmonise the many parts of life. To envisage such strategies, many taken for granted assumptions about how to work, how to care, about men and women's roles and about the roles and responsibilities of governments and organisations need to be questioned. This requires collaboration at all levels including individual, families, community and workplace levels, with support from governments and maybe even international organisations.

We now develop some more *possible* futures for some of our characters. What is potentially possible in each country will depend on particular histories, cultural factors and current challenges that different societies face. Different challenges such as HIV/AIDS, falling birth rates, rising levels of work-related sickness and stress or cultures of overwork may result in tipping points, which may ultimately push individuals, organisations and different societies to think much more radically about ways of harmonising the many parts of life in equitable, satisfying and sustainable ways. The resulting changes are likely to take different forms and occur in different ways.

---

[2] Even if women are compensated fully by government for staying at home – which is unlikely (Fraser, 1997) – it is likely that they will not be compensated sufficiently to experience similar living standards as men in retirement (see Rake, 1999, for a discussion of women, pensions and accumulated disadvantage in the cases of France, Germany and the UK).

Elizabeth and Enrika in the USA

So, what can we envisage for Elizabeth and Enrika in the USA? Looking back at the developments we charted in Chapter 2, we see most attention is given to paid work and personal life challenges at the workplace level. In our future scenarios, cultures of overwork, concerns about ageing populations and elder care needs, as well as mounting research and campaigning about the particular problems of low wage workers, are beginning to attract attention at state government levels. In particular, an innovative initiative promoted by a number of stakeholders to set up a work–family council at state level in the USA,[3] involving collaboration at multiple levels, is receiving increasing interest in other states.

Elizabeth is now a single mother with care of the elderly and childcare responsibilities and a demanding job. The company that she works for has become involved in setting up an initiative similar to the stakeholder forum that they have heard about at state level elsewhere. She becomes involved as an organisational representative. She is aware that this is taking up more of her time but feels this may potentially save her time in the long run. It is an investment she is prepared to make. Moreover, she feels that she is really benefiting from discussions with people from different backgrounds, including community leaders, family counsellors, trade unions and government policy makers. She is learning a great deal about the ways in which work–personal life challenges connect and interact at so many different levels.

Elizabeth becomes involved in a number of different initiatives. At her workplace, company executives give the go-ahead for work groups to discuss problems that current working practices are creating for their work and personal lives. With the help of action researchers, they plan experiments in different ways of working. The aim is to seek solutions that may help employees reduce their overload at work, and that enable them to harmonise their work and personal lives while enhancing – or at least not harming – workplace performance. Some groups find solutions that involve working more effectively. Others realise that their workloads are impossible and convince management of the need for more staff that will improve productivity in the long run.

At the work–family council discussions, trade union representatives continue to bring up the particular problems of low wage workers. Discussions increasingly focus on the need for state or federal government level policies to support these vulnerable people. At the workplace level, Elizabeth also begins to appreciate that low wage workers in her organisation face even more challenges than she does in managing their complex lives. So in their company initiatives, she pushes this agenda by constantly stressing that an action research process and new initiatives must include low skilled and temporary workers too.

One of the problems raised in these groups, and at the work–family forum, is the issue of childcare needs of low income parents, particularly those with non-standard and unpredictable work hours (see Henly & Lambert, 2004). In addition to looking at different ways that paid work might be organised to provide more predictability, it becomes apparent that community initiatives can also provide an important source of support for these families. Elizabeth does not have the time to get involved in community initiatives but mentions the scheme to Enrika. After consideration, Enrika discusses the possibility of looking after other people's children in the evenings or weekends when Elizabeth is at home. This could

---

[3] This idea emerged from a proposal written by academics in Massachusetts, which has resulted in a stakeholder group trying now to get state government level backing and support. Thank you to Professor Lotte Bailyn at MIT for alerting us to this innovation.

give Enrika more money to send home. Elizabeth and Enrika also begin to discuss work and personal life challenges more broadly and honestly with each other. They begin to talk about and think through possibilities of bringing Enrika's own children over to the USA with Elizabeth's support, or of Enrika job-sharing with her sister so that she can spend half the year with her children in the Philippines.[4]

These changes are all part of a larger process that will take time and meet with problems and resistances along the way. There are no concrete or one-size-fits-all solutions. Yet, as current and emerging resistances and challenges are considered, collaboration amongst people at multiple levels may yield new ideas and further developments.

Zhilah and Joseph in South Africa

What can we envisage for Zhilah and her husband, Joseph, in South Africa? In Chapter 2 we discussed the many social problems in South Africa. The spread of HIV/AIDS, high unemployment, growing backlash about boosting paid work opportunities for blacks and the need for economic development are top of the agenda. There is no question that things have to change. While harmonising work with other parts of life is not yet high on the agenda, changes triggered by other social forces are leading to connected discussions about social justice, care needs and quality of life.

In this South African future scenario, Zhilah leaves her job in the city and lives with her husband and her orphaned grandchildren. She is making good use of her time by becoming increasingly involved in the community, often taking care of other young children. Often their parents or carers cannot afford to give her money, but pay her in kind. Some give her local produce they have grown and others offer to make furniture for her. She reads a newspaper article about new local exchange trading systems (LETS) (Ouytsel & Vanderweyden, 2004) emerging in some countries: she laughs, this is already integral to people's survival here. She sees an opportunity: building on her experience of working in a bank, and her new contacts with community workers, she develops a proposal and secures government and international aid funding to develop care networks in her locality to formalize some of these LETS initiatives that are already taking place in her community. This attracts a lot of attention and begins to spread. She is able to use and develop some of the skills she has previously accumulated, and can also draw a small part-time salary for her work.

Meanwhile, trade union campaigns at the gold mine where Joseph works are beginning to focus on working practices and links with other parts of life. There has been much concern amongst employees about compulsory weekend work and increasingly long hours, especially among those who are affected by HIV/AIDS as sufferers or carers. A variety of leaves and flexible working practices are now being considered within the employer-equity forums, which have long been established by government. Now that Zhilah is bringing in some income, Joseph wants to reduce his hours at the gold mine and spend more time with his grandchildren. Many of his colleagues also want to change the ways they work: some want more work at the moment, others want less. Together, with support from their trade union representative, they are able to negotiate small changes at work that *begin* to reflect diverse needs of employees.

---

[4] These are only selected responses of course, and more radical ones may emerge.

These developments may seem small in the context of the huge problems South Africa faces. Yet, again, they reflect seeds of change that may grow and flourish over time.

Per and Siri in Norway

What can we envisage for Per and Siri in Norway? Norway has gone furthest at the social policy level in attempting to make the harmonisation of paid work with family responsibilities easier for men and women. Yet, as documented in Chapter 2, there is concern that stress, work intensification and global economic competition are undermining gender equality progress made so far. Associated pressures on women and men to have and do it all are being linked to rising divorce rates, sickness leaves and early retirement. These emerging concerns or social forces, in the context of considerable support for gender equality, may prompt further change at non-government levels.

Per has now left his demanding job and is working as a freelance consultant. This gives him more control over his time and he is getting on better with his wife, Siri. They now have much more time for each other. Siri still works at the same organisation, the one where Per had his bad experiences, which was discussed in Chapter 4. Since Per has gone freelance and been at home more, Siri has been able to increase her own working hours and is doing well at the company. Her role has developed to include responsibility for gender equality in the company. As she considers their policies and procedures she cannot but help reflect on what went wrong with Per's job. Why was his manager so unsupportive of the changes he made to his working practices? Is this a much more widespread problem?

Naturally, she begins to discuss this with colleagues at work and with Per at home, and to begin to reflect with others about where further changes are needed. There are good social and organisational policies in place, but there are many problems in practice. Managers are inconsistent in their implementation of policies, in their assumptions about men and women's commitment and notions of 'ideal' workers.

She develops a working group to look at the obstacles for further change. They agree that three things are important for bringing about change: legislation, working practices and the ways people think. Legislation is in place, and the company is already spearheading initiatives to look at working practices that enable greater equity between men and women. The daunting challenge now is to extend this focus to identity and relationship issues among men and women and how – and with what effect – this emerges in workplace contexts. The working group investigate work practice assumptions with conscious efforts to talk with men and women about their particular needs. This involves a long process of consultation and collaboration between men and women at different levels of the organisation. Men and women listen to each other, and this includes listening – and working through – perspectives of male managers that are resistant to supporting their male employees who want to radically change their working practices in ways that give them time for other parts of their lives, at the same time as not affecting workplace efficiency in negative ways.

These new initiatives also persuade Per to come back to the company in a consultancy position. The company benefits from the experience he has gained as a freelancer. Siri later becomes his line manager and they are comfortable with this: over the past few years they have been much more honest about their feelings with each other and are able to continually discuss challenges and problems as they arise.

When we leave this scenario people are still working on it but much progress has been made. Conversations prompt thinking about how men and women could work longer over the life course but less intensively at any one phase, particularly when they have other care or leisure commitments. These collaborative discussions are also spreading to family, friendship and community contexts. New collaborations and ideas are being explored.

Of course these are only a few of numerous possible future scenarios. They have limitations; we have been limited in our aspirations for change! We invite readers to consider other possibilities. These scenarios involve characters in their own countries finding individual solutions albeit working at different levels and bringing about some collective changes. There are some tenuous international links but they do not address global issues. Throughout the book we have emphasised the importance of recognising global connections. In particular, how the spread of neo-liberal capitalism is affecting working practices across the world, culminating in the invasiveness of paid work in more and more people's lives. Moreover, the outsourcing of work from developed to developing countries, with lower wages and poorer working conditions, undermines national government policies to support workers in harmonising paid work and the rest of life. It can stimulate the often discussed – but contested – 'race to the bottom' to see which countries can pay the least attention to social capital.[5] One challenge now is to envisage scenarios of international collaboration to address these global concerns. What will be the levers for change at this level? How will it come about? We hope that this book will stimulate thinking about change at the individual, family, workplace, community, national and global levels, to support ways of harmonising paid work and other parts of life that will provide benefits at all these levels.

SOME CONCLUDING REFLECTIONS

There are no easy quick fix solutions to the challenges explored in this book. We are only too aware that we have raised many more questions than we have answered. Our aim is not to prescribe but to stimulate wider and collaborative reflections.

What can be learnt from our possible scenarios? To conclude with a 'shopping list' of policy recommendations or prescriptive strategies for change at various levels would be futile and presumptuous. Different kinds of strategies for change go beyond policies and will vary depending on what is viewed as culturally acceptable and economically feasible in particular contexts. Nevertheless, there are some general points we would like to reiterate.

Fundamentally, changes that foster equitable, satisfying and sustainable opportunities for harmonising the many parts of people's lives have to occur at multiple levels.

At the level of national governments, supportive and enabling policies are crucial. They are important for protecting people, especially vulnerable groups, from the types of capitalism that put profits before social justice and quality of life. Progressive policies relat-

---

[5] At the same time, the idea of a 'race to the bottom' is also deeply debated. In the context of social policy, for example, see Alber and Standing (2000) for a critical overview and account. See also Sykes, Palier and Prior (2001) who argue that while changes are likely in different countries because of international and global forces, the extent and type of changes in particular countries will be mediated by national cultures and norms and so influence globalisation processes. Thus, they emphasise reciprocal and dynamic changes between international and national forces.

ing to working times, minimum wages, pay gaps between men and women, child and other forms of care, and family related leaves are all essential.[6] Additional policies at the workplace level can also be crucial. However, government and workplace policies, while necessary, do not bring about radical change unless supported by changes in practice and culture at multiple levels.

There is also a pressing need to work towards systemic change at the workplace as well as other levels. Systemic change involves challenging structures, cultures and practices. This will involve an ongoing process of reflection, collaboration and innovation, working continually with resistances and tensions as they arise. The challenge is to find ways of working that support harmonisations of paid work and personal life in ways that will not harm workplace effectiveness.

We have sought to demonstrate global connections in experiences of work and the rest of life, which is why many examples of process approaches used in this book are based on experiences in large organisations. However, we do not wish to perpetuate the myth that it is easier for larger than smaller organisations to make dual agenda changes. There are many examples of small organisations that have recognised that economic success and employee quality of life are crucially interrelated. Indeed, it can be easier to bring about systemic change in smaller organisations because it is easier to involve everyone in the change processes.[7]

There will nevertheless be some contexts where a business argument or even a dual agenda approach to change is not enough, and some ethical standards are needed. For example, there might be a good business argument for employing child labour but it is more or less universally agreed that this is not socially acceptable. Consideration of other international standards relating to the ways that people can harmonise the multiple parts of their lives in equitable, satisfying and sustainable ways are now crucial. Many trade unions are taking up these challenges and have an important role to play. In addition, corporate social responsibility agendas also need to take on these challenges. This may involve reflecting on bigger questions about what is enough profit or income, and weighing this against social justice and quality of life. There could be an important role for international organisations in setting standards in relation to corporate social responsibilities.

Another level in which action is needed is the community. The community has been described as the glue binding families and workplaces together. As we have seen in some of our stories, communities can provide essential support, sources of satisfaction and opportunities to address some of the bigger questions we have been raising in localised ways. Often some of the most innovative initiatives for change to support vulnerable or excluded people emerge at the community level. Dialogue between community groups and other levels of societies can feed into mutual learning and support.

The family is another important focus for change in collaboration with other levels of society. Changes in notions about 'ideal' workers, 'ideal' carers, or men and women's 'appropriate' roles in families, communities, workplaces and wider societies are all interdependent.

---

[6] For excellent accounts of policies that exist in various contexts in a range of 'developed' countries, and the impacts particular policy packages have on gender equity and child well-being, see Gornick and Meyers (2003); and Daly and Rake (2003). For a particular focus on fathers, Hobson (2002) offers a comprehensive account that takes in historical and contemporary trends in a selection of Nordic and Continental European countries as well as the UK and the USA. For a good summary and analysis of policy packages for lone mothers in different European countries, see Lewis (1998).

[7] For an example of such a process orientated approach in a small manufacturing company, see the organisational case study of Printco discussed in Lewis and Cooper (2005, pp. 71–85).

Individuals often blame themselves for what they see as their lack of ability to manage the invasiveness of paid work, to find time to give and receive care, or to challenge or escape from pervasive assumptions about how men and women should behave. While we have argued that change is essential at deeper levels of individual identity, it is clear that this cannot happen without related and collaborative changes at all other levels.

Challenges about how to combine paid work with other parts of life are not just individual problems, nor are they unrelated to wider social concerns. These challenges are linked to much bigger questions. This brings us back to the five Cs that we introduced in Part II. Underpinning all the challenges we have described are dominant or influential forms of neo-liberal *capitalism*, the lure of *consumerism* and particular ways of thinking about *commitment* that can combine to undermine *care* giving and receiving and a sense of *connectedness* with others. Yet, an emphasis on care, connectedness and diverse ways of thinking about commitment are essential for equity, well-being and sustainability.

To conclude, we add two more Cs. The first is *collaboration* at multiple levels as emphasised above. If people are not enabled to collaborate with others in ongoing reflections and actions, they are – to use the words of Robert Reich in our opening quote – left to grapple 'alone and in the dark'. None of this is easy. Challenges of harmonising paid work with the many parts of life touch on factors ranging from market structures, mentalities and constraints to deep identity anxieties and assumptions. Working through these challenges involves confronting many taboos and questioning seemingly unquestionable wisdoms at multiple and connected levels of society. If social justice, well-being and sustainability are valued, then, working towards more optimal changes is increasingly important and requires our final C: *courage*.

References

Alber, J. & Standing, G. (2000). Social dumping, catch-up or convergence? Europe in a comparative global context. *Journal of European Social Policy, 10*, 99–119.

Albrecht, G. (2003). How friendly are family friendly policies? *Business Ethics Quarterly, 13* (2), 177–193.

Allen, S. & Hawkins, A. (1999). Maternal gatekeeping: Mothers' beliefs and behaviours that inhibit greater father involvement in family work. *Journal of Marriage and the Family, 61* (1), 199–212.

Allen, T. (2001). Family supportive work environments: the role of organizational perceptions. *Journal of Vocational Behaviour, 58* (3), 453–468.

Anderson, T., Forth, J., Metcalf, H. & Kirby, S. (2001). *The Gender Pay Gap*, Report to the Women and Equality Unit. London: Cabinet Office.

Appelbaum, E. & Berg, P. (2001). High performance work systems and labor market structures. In Berg, I. & Kalleberg, A. L. (Eds.), *Sourcebook of Labor Markets*. New York: Kluwer.

Aryee, S. (2005). The Work-Family Interface in Urban Sub-Saharan Africa: A Theoretical Analysis. In Poelmans, S. (Ed.), *Work and Family: An International Research Perspective*. Mahwah, New Jersey: Lawrence Erlbaum Associates.

Bailyn, L. (1993). Breaking the Mould: women, men and time in the New Corporate World. New York: Free Press.

Bailyn, L. & Harrington, M. (2004). Redesigning work for work–family integration. In *Community, Work and Family, 7*, 199–211.

Barker, F. (2003). *The South African Labour Market* (4th ed.). Pretoria: Van Schaik.

Barnett, R. C. (1998). Towards a review and reconceptualisation of the work/family literature. *Genetic, Social and General Psychology Monographs, 24*, 125–182.

Barolsky, V. (2003). *Overextended: AIDS review 2003*. Pretoria: Centre for the Study of AIDS.

Bauman, Z. (1998). *Globalisation: The Human Consequences*. Cambridge: Polity Press.

Bauman, Z. (2003). *Liquid Love: On the Frailty of Human Bonds*. Cambridge: Polity Press.

Blau, F. D., Ferber, M. A. & Winkler, E. A. (2002). *The Economics of Women, Men and Work* (4th ed.). New Jersey: Prentice Hall.

Blunkett, D. (2001). *Politics and Progress: Renewing Democracy and Civil Society*. London: Politico's Publishing.

Bookman, A. (2004). *Starting in our Own Backyards: How Working Families can Build Community and Survive the New Economy*. New York: Routledge.

Bowlby, J. (1953). *Childcare and the Growth of Love*, Harmondsworth: Penguin.

Brandth, B. & Kvande, E. (2001). Flexible work and flexible fathers. *Work, Employment and Society, 15* (2), 251–267.

Brandth, B. & Kvande, E. (2002). Reflexive fathers: Negotiating parental leave and working life. *Gender, Work and Organization, 9* (2), 186–203.

Brannen, J. & Moss, P. (1998). The polarisation and intensification of parental employment in Britain: Consequences for parents, children and the community. *Community, Work and Family, 1* (3), 229–248.

Bryce, J. & Haworth, J. (2002). Well being and flow in a sample of male and female office workers. *Leisure Studies, 21*, 249–263.

Bunting, M. (2004). *Willing Slaves: How the Overwork Culture is Ruling our Lives*. London: Harpers and Collins.

Burchall, B., Lapido, D. & Wilkinson, F. (Eds.). (2002). *Job Insecurity and Work Intensification*. London: Routledge.

Burgess, A. & Russell, G. (2003). Fatherhood and public policy. *Supporting Fathers: Contributions from the International Parenthood Summit 2003*. Retrieved February 8, 2005, from Bernard van Leer Foundation, www.bernardvanleer.org.

Butler, A. & Skattebo, A. (2004). What is acceptable for women may not be for men: the effect of family conflicts with work on job performance ratings. *Journal of Occupational and Organizational Psychology, 77* (4), 553–564.

Castles, F. (2003). The world turned upside down: Below replacement fertility, changing preferences and family–friendly public policy in 21 OECD countries. *Journal of European Social Policy, 13* (3), 209–228.

Chabot, J. (1992). Dual-Earner Families and the Care of the Elderly. In Lewis, S., Izraeli, D. & Hootsmans, H. (Eds.), *Dual-Earner Families: International Perspectives*. London: Sage.

Chakrabarty, D. (2000). *Provincializing Europe: Postcolonial Thought and Historical Difference*. Princeton: Princeton University Press.

Clarke, J. (2004). *Changing Welfare, Changing States: New Directions in Social Policy*. London: Sage.

Connell, R. W. (1987). *Gender and Power: Society, the Person and Sexual Politics*. Cambridge: Polity Press.

Connell, R. W. (2001). The social organisation of masculinity. In Whitehead, S. & Barrett, F. (Eds.), *The Masculinities Reader*. Cambridge: Polity Press.

Connell, R. W. (2004). A Really Good Husband: Observations on work/life balance, gender justice and social change. Address to conference *Work–Life Balance Across the Life Course*, Edinburgh, June–July.

Cooke, L. P. (forthcoming, 2006). Le Sud Revisité: équité entre les Sexes et Fécondité en Italie et en Espagne (The South Revisited: Gender Equity and Fertility in Italy and Spain). *Research et Prévisions*.

Coppock, V., Haydon, D. & Richter, I. (1995). *The Illusions of 'Post-Feminism': New Women, Old Myths*. London: Taylor & Francis.

Cott, N. (1977). *The Bonds of Womanhood: 'Woman's Sphere' in New England, 1780–1835*. New Haven: Yale University Press.

Crompton, R. & Brockman, M. (2003). *Class, gender and work–life balance*. Paper presented at the ESRC Seminar Series on Work, Life and Time in the New Economy, London, May.

Crompton, R., Dennett, R. & Wigfield, A. (2003). *Organisations, Careers and Caring*. Bristol: Policy Press.

Csikszentmihalyi, M. (1997). *Finding Flow: The Psychology of Engagement with Everyday Life*. New York: Basic Books.

Curtis, R. (1986). Household and family in theory on inequality. *American Sociological Review, 51*, 168–163.

Dalley, G. (1996). *Ideologies of Caring*. London: Macmillan.

Daly, M. (1992). Europe's poor women: Gender in research on poverty. *European Sociological Review, 8*, 1–12.

Daly, M. & Rake, K. (2003). *Gender and the Welfare State*. Cambridge: Polity Press.

De Beauvoir, S. (1953). *The Second Sex* (H. M. Parshley, Trans. and Ed.). London: Jonathan Cape.

Degroot, J. & Fine, J. (2003). Integrating work and life: Young women forge new solutions. In Costello, C. B., Wight, V. R. & Stone, A. J. (Eds.), *The American Woman 2003–2004: Daughters of a Revolution – Young Women Today*. New York: Palgrave Press.

Delle Fave, A. & Massimini, F. (2003). Experiences in work and leisure among teachers and physicians and bio-cultural implications. *Leisure Studies, 22*, 323–342.

Demos, J. (1986). *Past, Present and Personal: The Family and the Life Course in American History*. New York: Oxford University Press.

Den Dulk, L. (2001). *Work–Family Arrangements in Organisations: A cross-national study in the Netherlands, Italy, the United Kingdom and Sweden*. Amsterdam: Rozenburg Publications.

Den Dulk, L. (2005). Workplace Work-Family Arrangements: A Study and Explanatory Framework of Differences between Organizational Provisions in Different Welfare States. In Poelmans, S. (Ed.), *Work and Family: An International Research Perspective*. Mahwah, New Jersey: Lawrence Erlbaum Associates.

Denzin, N. K. & Lincoln, Y. S. (Eds.). (1998). *Collecting and Interpreting Qualitative Materials*. London: Sage.

Devon, F. & Moss, P. (2002). Leave arrangements for parents: overview and future outlook. *Community, Work and Family*, 5 (3), 237–256.

Dewilde, C. (2002). The financial consequences of relationship dissolution for women in Western Europe. In Ruspini, E. & Dale, A. (Eds.), *The Gender Dimension of Social Change*. Bristol: The Policy Press.

Doolittle, M. (2004). Sexuality, parenthood and population: Explaining fertility decline in Britain from the 1860s to 1920s. In Carabine, J. (Ed.), *Sexualities: Personal Lives and Social Policy*. Bristol: Policy Press in association with The Open University.

Douglas, S. J. & Michaels, M. W. (2004). *The Mommy Myth: The Idealization of Motherhood and how it has Undermined Women*. New York: Free Press.

Dunne, G. A. (2000). Balancing acts: Lesbian experience of work and family life. In Sperling, L. & Owen, M. (Eds.), *Women and Work: The Age of Post-Feminism?* Aldershot: Ashgate.

Ehrenreich, B. & Hochschild, A. R. (2003). *Global Woman: Nannies, Maids and Sex Workers in the New Economy*. London: Granta.

Esping-Andersen, G. (1990). *The Three Worlds of Welfare Capitalism*. Cambridge: Polity Press.

Esping-Andersen, G. (2002). *Why We Need a New Welfare State*. Oxford: Oxford University Press.

Fagnani, J. (2004). *Transitions: Gender, Parenthood and the Changing European Workplace Context Mapping*. Manchester: RIHSC.

Ferguson, R. (2004). Remaking the relations of work and welfare. In Mooney, G. (Ed.), *Work: Personal Lives and Social Policy*. Bristol: Policy Press in association with The Open University.

Fink, J. (2004). *Care: Personal Lives and Social Policy*. Bristol: Polity Press in association with The Open University.

Fletcher, J. (1999). *Disappearing Acts: Gender, Power and Relational Practice at Work*. Cambridge, Massachusetts: MIT Press.

Flouri, E. (2005). *Fathering and Child Outcomes*. London: Wiley.

Fogarty, M., Rapoport, R. & Rapoport, R. N. (1971). *Sex, Career and Family*. London: Allen and Unwin.

Franks, S. (1999). *Having None of It. Women, Men and the Future of Work*. London: Granta.

Fraser, N. (1997). After the Family Wage: A Post Industrial Thought Experiment. In Fraser, N. (Ed.), *Justice Interuptus: Critical Reflections on the 'Post-Socialist' Condition*. New York: Routledge.

Friedan, B. (1963). *The Feminine Mystique*. London: Gollancz.

Frogett, L. (2002). *Love, Hate and Welfare: Psychosocial Approaches to Policy and Practice*. Bristol: Policy Press.

Frone, M. R., Yardley, J. K. & Markel, K. S. (1997). Developing and testing an integrative model of the work–family interface. *Journal of Vocational Behavior*, 50, 145–167.

Galinsky, E. (1998). Ask the children: what America's children really think about working parents. New York: William Morrow and Co.

Galinsky, E. Kim, S. & Bond, J. (2001). Feeling overworked: when work becomes to much. New York: Families and Work Institute.

Gallie, D. (2002). The quality of working life in welfare strategy. In Esping-Andersen, G. (Ed.), *Why we Need a New Welfare State*. Oxford: Oxford University Press.

Gauthier, A. H. (2005). Trends in policies for family-friendly societies. In Macura, M., MacDonald, A. L. & Haug, W. (Eds.), *The New Demographic Regimes: Population Challenges and Policy Responses*. New York: United Nations.

Gavron, H. (1966). *The Captive Wife: Conflicts of Housebound Mothers*. London: Routledge and K. Paul.

Gender Equality Bureau (2004). *Women in Japan Today*. Tokyo: Gender Equality Bureau, Cabinet Office.

Giddens, A. (1992). *The Transformation of Intimacy: Sexuality, Love and Eroticism in Modern Societies*. Oxford: Polity Press.

Giddens, A. (1999). *Runaway World: How Globalisation is Reshaping our Lives*. London: Profile.

Gornick, J. & Meyers, M. (2003). *Families That Work: Policies for Reconciling Parenthood and Employment*. New York: Russell Sage Foundation.

Gough, I. & Wood, G. (Eds.). (2004). *Insecurity and Welfare Regimes in Asia, Africa and Latin America*, Cambridge: Cambridge University Press.

Greer, G. (1971). *The Female Eunuch*. St Albans: Paladin.

Handy, C. (1997). *The Hungry Spirit: Beyond Capitalism: A Quest for Purpose in the Modern World.* London: Arrow, Random House.

Harker, L. & Lewis, S. (2001). Work–life policies: Where should the government go next? In Birkett, N. (Ed.), *A Life's Work: Achieving Full and Fulfilling Employment.* London: Institute of Public Policy Research (IPPR).

Harrington, M. (1999). *Care and Equality: Inventing a New Family Politics.* New York: Knopf.

Hartmann, H. (1979). Capitalism, patriarchy and job segregation by sex. In Eisenstein, Z. (Ed.), *Capitalist Patriarchy.* New York: Monthly Review Press.

Hawkins, A. J. & Dollahite, D. C. (Eds.). (1997). *Generative Fathering: Beyond Deficit Perspectives.* London: Sage.

Haworth, J. & Veal, A. (2005). *Work and Leisure.* Hove: Routledge.

Heilbrun, S., Heston, A. & Weiner, N. (Eds.). (1999). *The Annals of the American Academy of Political and Social Sciences: The Silent Crisis in US Childcare.* Thousand Islands, CA: Sage.

Henly, J. R. & Lambert, S. (2004). Non standard work and child-care needs of low income parents. In Bianchi, S., Casper, L. & King, R. (Eds.), *Work, Family, Health and Well-being.* Mahwah, New Jersey: Lawrence Erlbaum Associates.

Hertz, R. & Ferguson, R. (1998). Only one pair of hands: ways that single mothers stretch work and family resources. *Community, Work and Family, 1* (1), 13–38.

Hewitt, P. (1993). *About Time: The Revolution in Work and Family Life.* London: IPPR/Rivers Oram.

Heymann, J., Earle, A. & Hanchate, A. (2004). Bringing a global perspective to work and family: an examination of extended work hours in families in four countries. *Community, Work and Family, 7* (2), 247–272.

Hobson, B. & Morgan, D. (2002). Introduction. In Hobson, B. (Ed.), *Making Men into Fathers: Men, Masculinities and the Social Politics of Fatherhood.* Cambridge: Cambridge University Press.

Hobson, B. (Ed.). (2002). *Making Men into Fathers: Men, Masculinities and the Social Politics of Fatherhood.* Cambridge: Cambridge University Press.

Hochschild, A. R. (1983). *The Managed Heart: Commercialisation of Human Feeling.* Berkeley, CA: University of California Press.

Hochschild, A. R. (1997). *The Time Bind: When Work Becomes Home and Home Becomes Work.* New York: Henry Holt.

Hochschild, A. R. with Machung, A. (1989). *The Second Shift: Working Parents and the Revolution at Home.* London: Piatkus.

Holt, H. & Thaulow, I. (1996). Formal and informal flexibility in the workplace. In Lewis, S. & Lewis, J. (Eds.), *The Work–Family Challenge: Rethinking Employment.* London: Sage.

Iwao, S. (2003). *Gender, equality and family life.* Seminar given at the Daiwa Anglo-Japanese Foundation, London, September. see http://www.daiwa-foundation.org.uk/_pdf/Iwao%20transcript.pdf.

Jamieson, L. (1998). *Intimacy: Personal Relationships in Modern Societies.* Cambridge: Polity Press.

Kagan, C., Lewis, S. & Heaton, P. (1999). Enabled or disabled? Working parents of disabled children. *Journal of Community and Applied Psychology, 9,* 369–381.

Kamerman, S. & Kahn, A. (Eds.). (1997). *Family Change and Family Policies in Great Britain, Canada, New Zealand and the United States.* Oxford: Clarendon Press.

Keuzekamp, S. (2004). *Een EER voor de levenloopregeling.* The Hague: SCP and Ministry of Social Affairs and Employment.

Knijn, T. (2000). The rationalized marginalization of care: Time is money, isn't it? In Hobson, B. (Ed.), *Gender and Citizenship in Transition.* Basingstoke: Macmillan.

Knijn, T. (2003). Challenges and risks of individualisation in the Netherlands. *Social Policy and Society, 3* (1), 57–65.

Knijn, T. & Selten, P. (2002). Transformations of fatherhood: The Netherlands. In Hobson, B. (Ed.), *Making Men into Fathers: Men, Masculinities and the Social Politics of Fatherhood.* Cambridge: Cambridge University Press.

Kofman, E., Phyizacklea, A., Raghuram, P. & Sales, R. (2000). *Gender and International Migration in Europe: Employment, Welfare and Politics.* London: Routledge.

Lambert, S. (1999). Lower wage workers and the new realities of work and family. Annals AAPSS, *562,* 174–190.

Layard, R. (2003). *Happiness: Has Social Science A Clue?* Lionel Robbins Memorial Lectures, London: LSE.

Layard. R. (2005). *Happiness: Lessons from a New Science.* London: Allen Lane.

Leira, A. (1992). *Welfare States and Working Mothers: The Scandinavian Experience.* New York: Cambridge University Press.

Levine, J. & Pittinsky, T. L. (1997). *Working Fathers: New Strategies for Balancing Work and Family.* New York: Harcourt Brace.

Lewis, J. (1992). Gender and the developments of welfare regimes. *Journal of European Social Policy, 2* (3), 158–173.

Lewis, J. (Ed.). (1998). *Lone Mothers in European Welfare Regimes*: *Shifting Policy Logics.* London: Jessica Kingsley.

Lewis, J. (2001). The decline of the male breadwinner model: implications for work and care. *Social Politics, 8* (2), 159–162.

Lewis, J. (2002). The problem of fathers: Policy and behaviour in Britain. In Hobson, B. (Ed.), *Making Men into Fathers: Men, Masculinities and the Social Politics of Fatherhood.* Cambridge: Cambridge University Press.

Lewis, J. & Piachaud, D. (1987). Women and poverty in the twentieth century. In Glendinning, C. & Millar, J. (Eds.), *Women and Poverty in Britain.* Hemel Hempstead: Harvester Wheatsheaf.

Lewis, J., Kiernan, K. & Land, H. (1998). *Lone Motherhood in Twentieth-century Britain: From Footnote to Front Page.* New York: Clarendon Press.

Lewis, S. (1991). Motherhood and/or employment: the impact of social and organisational values. In Phoenix, A., Woollett, A. & Lloyd, E. (Eds.), *Motherhood; Meanings, Practices and Ideologies.* London: Sage.

Lewis, S. (1997). Family friendly policies: Organisational change or playing about at the margins? *Gender, Work and Organisations, 4,* 13–23.

Lewis, S. (2001). Restructuring workplace cultures: the ultimate work–family challenge? *Women in Management Review, 16* (1), 21–29.

Lewis, S. (2003a). Flexible working arrangements: implementation, outcomes and management. In Cooper, C. L. & Robertson, I. (Eds.), *International Review of Industrial and Organisational Psychology,* Vol. 18. London: Wiley.

Lewis, S. (2003b). The integration of paid work and the rest of life: Is post-industrial work the new leisure?. Leisure Studies, *22* (4), 343–355.

Lewis, S. & Cooper, C. (1999). The work–family research agenda in changing contexts. *Journal of Occupational Health Psychology, 4* (4), 382–393.

Lewis, S. & Cooper, C. (2005). *Work–Life Integration: Case Studies of Organisational Change.* London: Wiley.

Lewis, S. & Haas, L. (2005). Work–life integration and social policy: a social justice approach. In Kossek, E. & Lambert, S. (Eds.), *Work and Life Integration. Organizational, Cultural and Individual Perspectives.* Mahwah, New Jersey: Lawrence Erlbaum Associates.

Lewis, S. & Smithson, J. (2001). Sense of entitlement to support for the reconciliation of employment and family life. *Human Relations, 55* (11), 1455–1481.

Lewis, S., Kagan, C. & Heaton, P. (2000). Dual earner parents with disabled children: patterns for working and caring. *Journal of Family Issues, 21* (8), 1031–1060.

Lister, R. (1994). She has other duties – women, citizenship and social security. In Baldwin, S. & Falkingham, J. (Eds.), *Social Security and Social Change.* London: Harvester Wheatsheaf.

Lister, R. (2003). *Citizenship and Feminist Perspectives (2nd ed.).* New York: Palgrave Macmillan.

Lister, R. (2004). The Third Way's Social Investment State. In Lewis, J. & Surender, R. (Eds.), *Welfare State Change: Towards a Third Way.* Oxford: Oxford University Press.

MacInness, J. (1998). *The End of Masculinity: The Confusion of Sexual Genesis and Sexual Difference in Modern Society.* Buckingham: Open University Press.

Maree, J. & Godfrey, S. (2003). *If you can't measure it you can't manage it!: The Re-Organisation of Work and Employment as Managerial Strategies to Improve Performance at Two Fish Processing Firms.* Paper presented at the Sociology of Work Unit (SWOP) and The National Labour and Economic Development Institute (NALEDI) in association with the Harold Wolpe Memorial Trust conference, Work Restructuring in Post-Apartheid South Africa, Johannesburg, February.

Marks, S. R. (1977). Multiple roles and role strain: Some notes on human energy, time and commitment. *American Sociological Review*, *42*, 921–936.

Marshall, J. (1995). *Women Managers Moving On Exploring Career and Life Choices*. London: Routledge.

McGlynn, C. (2001). European Union family values: Ideologies of 'family' and 'motherhood' in European Union Law. *Social Politics*, *8*, 325–350.

Mitchell, J. (1966). Women: The longest revolution. *New Left Review*, 40, November/December.

Moen, P. & Sweet, S. (2004). From work–family to flexible careers; a life course reframing. *Community, Work and Family*, *7* (2), 209–226.

Moss, P. (2003). *The relationship between employment and care*. Paper presented at the Tedworth Seminar, Cumberland Lodge, October.

Myles, J. (2002). A new social contract for the elderly? In Esping-Andersen, G. (Ed.), *Why We Need a New Welfare State*. Oxford: Oxford University Press.

New York Times (2005). Forget the Career, My Parents Need Me at Home. By Jane Gross, November 24th.

O'Brien, M. (2005). *Shared Caring: Bringing Fathers into the Frame*, Working paper Series No. 18. London: Equal Opportunities Commission.

O'Brien, M. & Shemilt, I. (2003). *Working Fathers: Earning and Caring*. Manchester: Equal Opportunities Commission.

Oakley, A. (1974). *The Sociology of Housework*. London: Robertson.

OECD (1997). Sustainable Flexibility: A Prospective Study of Work, Family and Society in the Information Age. Paris: OECD.

OECD (2004). *Employment Outlook*. Paris: OECD.

Orloff, A. S. (1993). Gender and the social rights of citizenship: The comparative analysis of gender relations and welfare states. *American Sociological Review*, *58* (3), 303–328.

Ouytsel, J. V. & Vanderweyden, K. (2004). Do LETS Work? Weighing up Local Exchange Trading Systems and wage labour. *Community, Work and Family*, *7* (1), 71–94.

Pahl, J. (1989). *Money and Marriage*. Basingstoke: Macmillan.

Pahl, R. (2000). *On Friendship*. Cambridge: Polity Press.

Parris, M. A., Vickers, M. H. & Wilkes, L. (2005). Fitting Friendships into the Equation: Middle managers and the work/life balance. Conference paper presented at the *Gender, Work and Organisation 4th International Interdisciplinary Conference*, Keele University, Staffordshire, UK, June 22–24.

Pateman, C. (1988). *The Sexual Contract*. Cambridge: Polity Press.

Pearson, A. (2003). *I Dont Know How She Does It: A Comedy of Failure, a Tragedy of Success*. London: Vintage.

Perlow, L. A. (1998). Boundary control: the social ordering of work and family time in a high tech organisation. *Administrative Science Quarterly*, *43*, 328–357.

Perrons, D. (2003). The new economy and the work life balance. A case study of the new media sector in Brighton and Hove. *Gender, Work and Organisation*, *10* (1), 65–93.

Phillipson, C. (1996). Intergenerational conflict and the welfare state: American and British perspectives. In Walker, A. (Ed.), *The New Generational Contract*. London: University College London Press.

Pleck, J. H., & Masciadrelli, B. P. (2003). Paternal involvement: Levels, sources, and consequences. In Lamb, M. E. (Ed.), *The Role of the Father in Child Development* (4th ed.), New York: John Wiley.

Poarch, M. T. (1998). Ties that bind: US suburban residents and the social and civic dimensions of work. *Community, Work and Family*, *1* (2), 125–147.

Poster, W. (2005). Organisational change, globalisation and work-family programs: Case studies from India and the United States. In Poelmans, S. (Ed.), *Work and Family: An International Research Perspective*. Mahwah, New Jersey: Lawrence Erlbaum Associates.

Pruitt, B. & Rapoport, R. (2003). Looking Backwards to Go Forward: A Timeline of the Work-Family Field in the United States since World War II. Retrieved February, 2005, from http://www.bc.edu/bc_org/avp/wfnetwork/timelines/.

Putnam, R. (2000). *Bowling Alone: The Collapse and Revival of American Community*. New York: Simon & Schuster.

Rajdhyahsha & Smita (2004). *Tracing a timeline for work and family research in India*. Retrieved February, 2005, from http://www.bc.edu/bc_org/avp/wfnetwork/timelines/.

Raju, S. & Bagchi, D. (Eds.). (1993). *Women and Work in Asia: Regional Patterns and Perspectives*. London: Routledge.

Rake, K. (1999). Accumulated disadvantage. In Clasen, J. (Ed.), *Comparative Social Policy: Concepts, Theories and Methods*. Oxford: Blackwell.

Ramu, G. N. (1987). Indian husbands: Their role perception and performance in single and dual-earner families. *Journal of Marriage and the Family, November*, 903–915.

Rani, K. (1976). *Role Conflict in Working Women*. New Delhi: Chetana.

Rapoport, R. & Rapoport, R. N. (1965). Work and family in contemporary society. *American Sociological Review, 30* (3), 381–394.

Rapoport, R. & Rapoport, R. N. (1971). *Dual-Career Families*. London: Penguin.

Rapoport, R. & Rapoport, R. N. (1975). Men, women and equity. *Family Coordinator, 24* (4), 421–432.

Rapoport, R. & Rapopot, R. N. (1975). Leisure and the family life cycle. London: Routledge and Kegen Paul.

Rapoport, R., Bailyn, L., Kolb, D. & Fletcher, J. (1996). *Relinking Life and Work*. Pegasus Communications: Innovations in Management Series. Massachusetts: Pegasus Communications.

Rapoport, R., Bailyn, L., Fletcher, J. & Pruitt, B. (2002). *Beyond Work–Family Balance: Advancing Gender Equity and Work Performance*. London: Wiley.

Rapoport, R., Lewis, S. & Gambles, R. (2005). Work–personal life integration: visions and pragmatic strategies for change. In Lewis, S. & Cooper, C. (Eds.), *Work–Life Integration: Case Studies of Organisational Change*. London: Wiley.

Reich, R. (2001). *The Future of Success*. New York: Knopf.

Remery, C., Schippers, J. & Van Doorne-Huiskes, A. (2002). *Zorg als arbeidsmarktgegeven: werkgevers ann zet*. Tilburg: Organisatie voor Strategisch Arbeidsmarktonderzoek.

Rosenfeld, A. & Wise, N. (2000). *The Over-scheduled Child: Avoiding the Hyper-parenting Trap*. New York: St. Martin's Press.

Royal Commission on Long Term Care (1999). *With Respect to Old Age: Long Term Care – Rights and Responsibilities*. Retrieved March, 2005, from http://www.archive.official-documents.co.uk/document/cm41/4192/v1ch6.pdf.

Sabo, D. & Gordon, S. (1995). Rethinking men's health and illness. In Sabo, D. & Gordon, D. (Eds.), *Men's Health and Illness: Gender, Power and the Body*. London: Sage.

Said, E. (1993). *Culture and Imperialism*. London: Chatto.

Sainsbury, D. (1994). Women and Men's Social Rights: Gendering Dimensions of Welfare States. In Sainsbury, D. (Ed.), *Gendering Welfare States*. London: Sage.

Sainsbury, D. (2001). Gender and the making of welfare states: Norway and Sweden. *Social Politics, 8*, 113–143.

Schaapman, M. (1995). *Ongezien onderscheid. Een analyse van de verborgen machtswerking van sekse*. Den Haag: Ministerie van Sociale zaken en Werkgelegenheid/VUGA.

Schor, J. (1998). The Overspent American: Upscaling, Downshifting and the New Consumer. New York: Basic Books.

Scott, J. (1996). *Only Paradoxes to Offer: French Feminists and the Rights of Man*. Harvard: Harvard University Press.

Sekaran, U. (1984). Job and life satisfaction experienced by dual-career family members. *Journal of Psychological Research, 28* (3), 139–144.

Sekaran, U. (1992). Middle-class dual-earner families and their support systems in urban India. In Lewis, S., Izraeli, D. & Hootsmans, H. (Eds.), *Dual-Earner Families: International Perspectives*. London: Sage.

Sennett, R. (1998). *The Corrosion of Character: The Personal Consequences of Work in the New Capitalism*. New York: Norton.

Sevenhuijsen, S. (1998). *Citizenship and the Ethics of Care: Feminist Considerations on Justice, Morality, and Politics*. London: Routledge.

Silverman, D. (2001). *Interpreting Qualitative Data: Methods for analysing talk, text and interaction* (2nd ed.). London: Sage.

Smithson, J. (2005). Full timer in a part time job: Identity negotiation in organisational talk. *Feminism and Psychology, 15* (3), 275–293.

Smithson, J., Lewis, S., Cooper, C. & Dyer, J. (2004). Flexible working and the gender pay gap in the accountancy profession. *Work, Employment and Society, 18* (1), 115–135.

Sparks, K., Cooper, C., Fried, Y. & Shirom, A. (1997). The effects of hours of work on health: a meta-analytic review. *Journal of Occupational Psychology*, *70*, 391–408.

Stanley, K. (Ed.). (2005). *Active Fathering*. London: IPPR.

Stiglitz, J. (2002). Globalisation and its Discontents. London: Allen Lane.

Sykes, R., Palier, B. & Prior, P. (Eds.). (2001). *Globalisation and European Welfare States*. Basingstoke: Palgrave.

Thompson, C. A. (1999). When work–family benefits are not enough: the influence of work–family culture on benefit utilization, organizational attitudes and work–family conflict. *Journal of Vocational Behaviour*, *54*, 392–415.

Tosh, J. (1999). *A Man's Place: Masculinity and the Middle Class Home in Victorian England*. Bath: Bath Press.

Toynbee, P. (2003). *Hard Work: Life in Low Pay Britain*. London: Bloomsbury.

Transition Research Report #1 (2003). Context Mapping, for the EU Framework 5 study 'Gender, Parenthood and the Changing European Workplace'. Retrieved February, 2005, from www. workliferesearch.org/transitions.

Transitions Research Report #3 (2004). *Gender, Parenthood and the Changing European Workplace*. Case studies report for the EU Framework 5 funded study. Manchester: Manchester Metropolitan University.

Tronto, J. (1993). *Moral Boundaries: A Political Argument for an Ethic of Care*. London: Routledge.

United Nations (1999). *The Invisible Heart – Care and the Global Economy. Human Development Report 1999*. Oxford: Oxford University Press.

Van de Bogard, J., Collins, I. & Van Iren, A. (2003). *On Linking Quality of Work and Life*. The Hague, Netherlands: Ministry of Social Affairs and Employment.

Van Niekerk, R. (2003). The evolution of health and welfare policies in South Africa: Inherited institutions, fiscal restraint, and the deracialization of social policy in the post-apartheid era. *The Journal of African American History*, *88* (4), 361–376.

Voydanoff, P. (2004). Implications of work and community demands on family integration. *Journal of Family and Economic Issues*, *25*, 7–23.

Webster, J. (2004). Working and living in the knowledge society: the policy implications of developments in working life and their effects on social relations. Report for the *Infowork: Social Cohesion, the organisation of work and information and communication technologies: drawing out the lessons of the TSER research programme and the Key Action on Socio-economic Research*, Brussels.

West, C. & Zimmerman, D. (1987). Doing gender. *Gender and Society*, *1* (2), 125–151.

White, M., Hill, S., McGovern, P., Mills, C. & Smeaton, D. (2003). High performance management practices, working hours and work–life balance. *British Journal of Industrial Relations*, *41* (2), 175–195.

Whitehouse, G., Zetlin, D. & Earnshaw, J. (2001). Prosecuting pay equity: Evolving strategies in Britain and Australia. *Gender, Work and Organization*, *8* (4), 365–386.

Williams, F. (2001). In and beyond New Labour: Towards a political ethic of care. *Critical Social Policy*, *21* (4), 467–493.

Williams, F. (2004). *Rethinking Families*. London: Calouste Gulbenkian Foundation.

Wilson, G. (2000). *Understanding Old Age: Critical and Global Perspectives*. London: Sage.

Winnicott, D. (1968). *The Family and Individual Development*. London: Tavistock Publications.

Winsom, A. & Leach, B. (2002). *Contingent Work, Disrupted Lives: Labour and Community in the New Rural Economy*. Toronto: University of Toronto Press.

Woodward, K. (Ed.). (2000). *Questioning Identity: Gender, Class, Nation*. London: Routledge.

Worrall, L. & Cooper, C. L. (2001). *Quality of Working Life: 2000 Survey of Managers' Changing Experiences*. London: Institute of Management.

Zuzanek, J. (2005). Work, leisure, time pressure and stress. In Haworth, J. T. & Veal, A. J. (Eds.), *Work and Leisure*. Hove: Routledge.

Index